THE
DRUG
PROBLEM

AMERICAN ISSUES

DEBATED

THE
DRUG
PROBLEM

Herbert M. Levine

RSVP

RAINTREE
STECK-VAUGHN
PUBLISHERS
The Steck-Vaughn Company

Austin, Texas

For Martin and Sylvia Gingold

Published by Raintree Steck-Vaughn Publishers, an imprint of Steck-Vaughn Company
Publishing Director: Walter Kossmann
Graphic Design & Project Management: Gino Coverty
Editors: Kathy DeVico, Shirley Shalit
Photo Editor: Margie Foster
Electronic Production: Gino Coverty

Library of Congress Cataloging-in-Publication Data
Levine, Herbert M.
The drug problem / Herbert M. Levine.
p. cm.—(American issues debated)
Includes bibliographical references and index.
ISBN 0-8172-4354-2
1. Drug abuse--United States.   I. Title.   II. Series.
HV5825.L444   1998
362.29'0973--dc21   97-17074
                                    CIP
                                    AC

Printed and bound in the United States
1 2 3 4 5 6 7 8 9 0 LB 01 00 99 98 97

Photograph Acknowledgments
p. 7 AP Photo/The News Review, Christian Murdock; p. 9 © Stephen Schapiro/Gamma Liason; p. 14 © Luc Novovitch/Gamma Liason; p. 18 © John Chiasson/Gamma Liason; p. 24 Courtesy The National Inhalant Prevention Coalition; p. 26 © Zigy Kaluzny/Tony Stone Images, Inc.; p. 28 © Diana Walker/ Gamma Liason; p. 36 © Georges Merillon/Gamma Liason; p. 38 UPI/Corbis-Bettmann; p. 43 Reuters/ Corbis-Bettmann; p. 45 © Stephen Ferry/Gamma Liason; p. 51 Culver Pictures; p. 52 UPI/Corbis-Bettmann; p. 56 AP·Photo/Gary I. Rothstein; p. 59 UPI/Corbis-Bettmann; p. 63 Reuters/Corbis-Bettmann; p. 71 AP Photos/Columbus Dispatch, Jeff Hinckley; p. 75 © Paul S. Howell/Gamma Liason; p. 78 The Bettmann Archive; p. 81 Reuters/Corbis-Bettmann; p. 86 © Craig Filpacchi/Gamma Liason; p. 88 © Brad Markel/Gamma Liason; p. 90 © Mark Richards/PhotoEdit; p. 92 © Michael Newman/ PhotoEdit; p. 93 AP Photo/Karin Cooper; p. 95 © Jeff Greenberg/PhotoEdit; p. 98 © Wisser/Gamma Liason; p. 103 Reuters/Corbis-Bettmann; p. 107 © Ed Lallo/Liason International; p. 109 UPI/Corbis-Bettmann; p. 113 Reuters/Gretta Pratt/Archive Photos.

CONTENTS

Chapter 1
INTRODUCTION: THE USE OF DRUGS

The United States is a nation of drug takers. Americans eat, drink, inject, smoke, and inhale more drugs than do people from any other nation in the world. They also spend more money on drugs that affect the mind or mental processes than any other people. Some drugs that Americans use are legal, healthy, and truly help people to prevent or cure illness and relieve pain. Common drugs that can be purchased without a doctor's prescription, like aspirin and cold tablets, are everyday examples. And drugs prescribed by doctors have saved or lengthened the lives of people with many serious ailments, including cancer, heart disease, and arthritis. Were it not for drugs developed mostly in the 20th century, millions of people throughout the United States and the rest of the world would suffer and die from diseases such as polio, yellow fever, influenza, pneumonia, and dysentery.

Just because a drug is legal, however, does not mean that it is used in a manner that improves health. Some people obtain prescriptions of powerful legal drugs that are psychoactive (affect the mind and mental processes) and overuse those drugs in a way that damages their health. And some nonprescription items, such as tobacco and alcohol, that can be purchased legally in most parts of the United

States, contain substances that can cause liver damage, cancer, heart disease, and early death.

But some drugs that Americans consume are illegal because they are a direct threat to the good health and well-being of the people who take them as well as an indirect threat to the safety of innocent people who do not. These illegal drugs may not only shorten the lives of the people who use them but may also destroy minds, make people suffer, prevent them from working, wreck families, and turn innocent people into criminals who steal property, rape, assault, or kill. This book focuses on these illegal drugs. As used in this book, the term "drugs" generally refers to illegal substances.

A number of surveys show the extent of drug use in America. The Substance Abuse and Mental Health Services Administration (SAMHSA), a federal agency in the Department of Health and Human Services (HHS), disclosed on the basis of its 1994 *National Household Survey on Drug Abuse* that 72 million (34.4 percent) of Americans aged 12 and older reported some use of an illicit

The number of juveniles charged with narcotics-related crimes in the United States more than doubled between 1990 and 1995.

(unlawful) drug at least once during their lifetime, 10.8 percent reported use during the past year, and 6 percent reported use in the month before the survey was conducted.

Teenage use of illegal drugs has been rising since 1992. According to *Monitoring the Future*, an annual federally funded survey, between

1995 and 1996, the percentage of eighth graders who said they used any kind of illegal drug in the past year increased from 21.4 percent to 23.6 percent. Among tenth graders, the rate rose from 33.3 percent to 37.5 percent. Among twelfth graders, the rate went from 39 percent to 40.2 percent. The leading illegal drug use was marijuana. And Federal Bureau of Investigation (FBI) crime studies show that the number of juveniles charged with narcotics-related crimes in the United States more than doubled between 1990 and 1995—from 64,740 in 1990 to 147,107 in 1995.

Although 72 million Americans have experimented with illegal drugs, the overwhelming majority of them have quit using illegal drugs as a result of their own decisions. Hard-core drug users are the biggest problem that the nation faces in dealing with drugs. They use the largest share of illegal drugs in the United States. For example, two-thirds of the nation's supply of cocaine (a drug made from the coca leaf) is consumed by about one-quarter of the total number of cocaine users.

Most Americans oppose the use of illegal drugs. The widespread use of drugs is of concern to many Americans because of the enormous economic and social consequences that drug use produces. According to the Office of National Drug Control Policy (ONDCP), the White House agency that coordinates the federal government's antidrug policies, in 1993 alone, Americans spent an estimated $49 billion on illegal drugs. The annual cost to society for dealing with the effects of drug use is $67 billion, mostly from the consequences of crime. Americans are well aware of the vast scale of drug use. According to a Gallup Poll, almost one-half (45 percent) of Americans report that either they, someone in their family, or a close friend has used illegal drugs. Of these, 28 percent described the drug use as moderate, while 29 percent described it as serious.

It is when drugs claim the lives of some of the nation's most prominent figures that Americans focus intently on the dangers of these illicit substances. Charlie Parker, a leader of the bop movement in jazz, was a heroin addict and died in 1955 at the age of 34. John

Belushi, a popular entertainer on television and in the movies, died at the age of 33 in 1982 from a combination of heroin and cocaine. Len Bias, the University of Maryland basketball star, died on June 17, 1986, while he was celebrating his signing of a contract to play professional basketball with the Boston Celtics. A few weeks later, Don Rogers, a Cleveland Browns defensive back, dropped dead from cocaine poisoning. The list of celebrities who died prematurely because of drug overdoses is long and sad and includes Elvis Presley, Janis Joplin, and River Phoenix.

The young actor River Phoenix died of a drug overdose on October 31, 1993.

History

The use of drugs on what is now the territory of the United States has a long history. Native Americans in North America used peyote, an organic hallucinogen (a drug that affects perception, sensation, and emotion; also known as a psychedelic, a substance that causes hallucinations), as part of religious rites. In the 19th century, doctors prescribed opium and morphine regularly to relieve pain or tension. Morphine was used on troops to treat painful wounds in the American Civil War. Some estimates say that 400,000 soldiers became addicted in this manner.

When cocaine appeared in the 1880s, it was welcomed for its healing powers. In the late 19th century, many products sold as syrups and cures for ailments, such as headaches, toothaches, depression, and alcoholism, contained opiates (substances made from the opium poppy) and/or cocaine. As people who took these products developed a dependency on them and could not bear to live without them, doctors soon understood the dangers of opiates and cocaine and advised their patients accordingly. In 1900, there were more narcotics addicts, proportionate to the population, than there are today. But most of them were medical addicts, who used drugs for their health, rather than recreational addicts, who used drugs for their pleasure. Women were the largest group of addicts in the late 19th century because they were heavy users of patent medicines (medicines that could be obtained without a prescription) and cocaines, which were regarded as medicines at the time.

Some people, particularly in the entertainment world, continued to use drugs in the 1920s and 1930s, and after World War II, as well. But a new turn in drug use took place in the 1960s as a result of publicity from individuals who rejected traditional values and became rebellious against society. Sparked by poet Allen Ginsberg, writer Jack Kerouac, writer Ken Kesey, and psychologist Timothy Leary, this counterculture movement, as it was called, supported illegal drug use. Leary, a Harvard University professor, was thrown out of Harvard in 1963 when it was discovered that undergraduates had shared in Leary's supply of drugs. Leary argued that LSD (lysergic acid diethylamide), a powerful synthetic drug that affects the feelings of the user, is not harmful and actually improves the functioning of the brain. The drug users of the counterculture were largely white and middle class. They actively celebrated drug-taking as a way of reaching a higher way of thinking than a "straight" person (one who does not depart from established acceptable behavior and who does not use drugs) experiences.

The counterculture lost its popular appeal as drugs destroyed victims who had accepted their presumed delights. In addition, the widespread publicity from the devastation caused by crack (an inexpensive form of cocaine) and from the transmission of Acquired Immunodeficiency Syndrome (AIDS), a disease that attacks the body's immune system and is usually fatal, as a result of the sharing of hypodermic needles used to inject drugs, took much of the glamour out of drugs.

In the 1960s and 1970s, Americans experienced a drug problem as a result of U.S. involvement in the Vietnam War. Heroin became available in Laos, Burma, and Thailand during the Vietnam War and was supplied by dealers in great amounts to U.S. soldiers fighting in that war. President Richard Nixon's administration took steps to help the soldiers who had become heroin users. Under his administration's program, the U.S. military tested for drug use all American military personnel who were leaving Vietnam for the United States. Those who tested positive remained overseas for treatment to ensure that they returned to the United States drug-free.

Millions of Americans continue to use illegal drugs. But American society frowns on such behavior. Government agencies and private companies make avoidance of drugs a condition of employment. Schools expel or suspend students and deny them the opportunity to compete as athletes when they are found to use or distribute drugs. What support exists for drug use in American society comes not from an acceptance of the views of the counterculture but rather from pleas coming from figures in public life who argue that the war on drugs produces more harm than the drugs themselves. (See Chapter 4.) But most of these figures condemn the use of drugs and warn about its great dangers.

Government Regulation

Because drugs can do so much harm to people, government has tried to regulate them. The early attempts to deal with drugs in the United States came not from the federal government, however, but rather from state and local governments. In 1860, for example, Pennsylvania passed an antimorphine law. In 1875, San Francisco adopted the first antidrug law in the United States that was directed against places in which people gathered to take opium.

Modern federal drug control legislation began with an 1887 law prohibiting the importation of smoking opium by Chinese immigrants. However, under this law, American citizens could and did continue to import opium. In 1909, federal legislation outlawed the smoking of opium. The United States was one of many nations that signed the Hague Opium Convention of 1912 that called for controlling opiates and cocaine. The enactment of the Harrison Narcotic Act of 1914 (named for Democratic congressman Francis Burton

Harrison of New York City) was a fulfillment of the U.S. obligation under the international convention. The law regulated traffic in narcotics and other drugs. It required doctors and pharmacists to keep records of drug distribution and also required the purchase of tax stamps to ensure government supervision of drug sales.

Marijuana was not covered in the Harrison Act. The first concern about marijuana came as a result of its use by Mexican immigrant workers in the South and the West. In 1915, Congress banned its importation except for medical purposes. Marijuana was not included in the Harrison Act because of its medical use in treatments for migraine (severe headache) and glaucoma (an eye disease). By 1937, every state had declared marijuana to be illegal. In 1937, Congress passed the Marijuana Tax Act. The law placed a one-dollar tax per ounce of marijuana on anyone who grew, transported, sold, prescribed, or used marijuana and required everyone who did so to register. Although the federal law did not specifically state that marijuana was illegal, it had that effect because the states had made the product illegal and failure to register was now a federal offense.

Congress passed the Controlled Substances Act in 1970, which brought together existing laws and regulations on drugs. It changed the system of penalties for drug violations and increased the regulation of medicinal drugs. It created five schedules of dangerous drugs. These schedules are governmental lists of groups or categories of drugs subject to legal controls or restrictions. Schedule I drugs have no acceptable medical use in the United States and cannot be prescribed. They may be used for research purposes, but only after special application is made to federal agencies. Schedule II drugs may be used for medical purposes, but they are regarded as dangerous because they can produce psychological (relating to the mind) and physiological (relating to the functioning of the body) dependencies. Physicians must be registered with the Drug Enforcement Administration (DEA), the federal agency charged with responsibility for enforcing federal drug laws, and follow appropriate procedures to use Schedule II drugs. Schedules III, IV, and V drugs can be used for medical purposes. They are less likely than Schedules I and II drugs to lead to dependency. (See Table 1.1.) As the table shows, heroin and marijuana are in Schedule I. Cocaine and morphine are in Schedule II.

Table 1.1

Drugs of Abuse Under the Controlled Substances Act

Schedule I
- The drug or other substance has a high potential for abuse.
- The drug or other substance has no currently accepted medical use in treatment in the United States.
- There is a lack of accepted safety for use of the drug or other substance under medical supervision.
- Some Schedule I substances are heroin, LSD, marijuana, and methaqualone.

Schedule II
- The drug or other substance has a high potential for abuse.
- The drug or other substance has a currently accepted medical use in treatment in the United States or a currently accepted medical use with severe restrictions.
- Abuse of the drug or other substance may lead to severe psychological or physical dependence.
- Schedule II substances include morphine, PCP, cocaine, methadone, and methamphetamine.

Schedule III
- The drug or other substance has a potential for abuse less than the drugs or other substances in Schedules I and II.
- The drug or other substance has a currently accepted medical use in treatment in the United States.
- Abuse of the drug or other substance may lead to moderate or low physical dependence or high psychological dependence.
- Anabolic steroids, codeine and hydrocodene with aspirin or Tylenol, and some barbiturates are Schedule III substances.

Schedule IV
- The drug or other substance has a low potential for abuse relative to the drugs or other substances in Schedule III.
- The drug or other substance has a currently accepted medical use in treatment in the United States.
- Abuse of the drug or other substance may lead to limited physical dependence or psychological dependence relative to the drugs or other substances in Schedule III.
- Included in Schedule IV are Darvon, Talwin, Equanil, Valium, and Xanax.

Schedule V
- The drug or other substance has a low potential for abuse relative to the drugs or other substances in Schedule IV.
- The drug or other substance has a currently accepted medical use in treatment in the United States.
- Abuse of the drug or other substance may lead to limited physical dependence or psychological dependence relative to the drugs or other substances in Schedule IV.
- Over-the-counter cough medicines with codeine are classified in Schedule V.

Source: Drug Enforcement Agency, *Drugs of Abuse: 1996*

Since 1984, Congress has included drug-related provisions in five major anticrime bills: the Crime Control Act of 1984, the Anti-Drug Abuse Act of 1986, the Anti-Drug Abuse Act of 1988, the Crime Control Act of 1990, and the Violent Crime Control and Law Enforcement Act of 1994. These laws have added penalties for drug crimes, expanded the role of the federal government in fighting drugs, increased funding for antidrug programs, and improved coordination among federal agencies in the war on drugs.

Today, federal and state drug laws cover a broad scope of prohibitions. Possession or use laws prohibit having a controlled drug on one's person or under one's control, such as in one's car or house. Manufacturing prohibitions include any activity related to the production of illegal drugs, such as the cultivation and harvest of drug-related plants, processing of certain chemicals, production of the substance, and preparation and packaging for distribution.

Police display drug paraphernalia seized in a raid.

Some laws cover illegal activities related to drug possession and trafficking. These include laws dealing with drug paraphernalia, precursor chemicals, money laundering, organized crime, and driving while intoxicated. Drug paraphernalia laws prohibit the possession or sale of articles used to administer illegal drugs although the articles may not be otherwise illegal. Precursor chemical laws regulate the chemicals that can be used in processing illegal drugs. Money-laundering laws make it a crime to convert money obtained through illegal means into money that appears to have come from a legal source in an attempt to avoid detection by government authorities. Organized crime laws, such as the Racketeer Influenced and Corrupt Organizations (RICO) laws, provide penalties for drug distribution that takes place as part of a criminal enterprise. And driving while intoxicated laws apply to both alcohol and drugs.

Federal Agencies and Drugs

Many federal agencies are involved in drug matters. As mentioned on page 8, the ONDCP in the White House coordinates the federal antidrug programs. Its leader is sometimes known as the drug "czar" (someone who has great authority in a particular area). Every year, ONDCP issues a national drug-control strategy report. The DEA, FBI, and Bureau of Prisons in the Department of Justice play central law-enforcement roles. HHS, Veterans Affairs, and the Justice Department have programs for drug treatment. Both the Departments of Education and HHS carry out drug-prevention programs.

Mostly since the 1980s, the Department of Defense (DOD) has played an increasingly important role in providing detection and other support in the war on drugs. The Customs Service, the Immigration and Naturalization Service (INS), and the Coast Guard work to stop drugs from entering the United States. The State Department, Central Intelligence Agency (CIA), and the U.S. Agency for International Development (AID) play international roles. And state and local agencies and courts play a vital role in drug matters, too.

Although most Americans are opposed to the use of illegal drugs, they differ about the purpose, wisdom, and methods used in dealing with illegal drugs. Some of the most important differences focus on the effectiveness of policies designed to stop drugs from coming into the United States, the necessity of making drug use a criminal offense, the role of drug policy in civil liberties, the effect of drug policy on racial minorities, and the fairness of drug tests. The debates in this book consider the pros and cons of these issues. But an understanding of the issues requires, first, some basic facts about what drugs are, what they do, and how people who are addicted to drugs can be treated.

Chapter 2
DRUGS OF ABUSE: A PORTRAIT

A drug is a chemical substance that causes some effect on a living thing. An individual who takes drugs may develop a drug dependence. Dependence means needing to take a drug regularly either to prevent physiological symptoms, which affect the body, or psychological symptoms, which affect the mind. Withdrawal, a period during which an addict stops taking drugs, usually marked by nausea, chills, vomiting, muscular pains and cramps, and running nose, is a physiological symptom. Feeling that one needs a drug to "get through the day" is a psychological symptom. With heroin users, the body requires regular doses of heroin and reacts violently if none is taken. With cocaine, the dependence is more psychological. There may be illusions of increased mental and physical strength. Or there may be hallucinations—false perceptions of reality or delusions.

When a person develops a compulsive use of a drug or other substance known by the user to be harmful, he or she is said to have an addiction to the substance. This condition arises when a person builds up a tolerance for a drug, which is a state in which the body becomes less responsive to a specific drug and so has a need for increasing doses of that drug in order to get a "high" feeling (a state of excitement, intoxication, or great happiness). The point at which a person becomes addicted to a drug varies from individual to individual and from substance to substance.

When a person takes a drug in a manner that harms that individual and may also harm others, then the person is said to be engaging in drug abuse. People often think that they can control their use of a strong drug, such as cocaine or heroin, but they find to their regret that they become addicted to it. In tests of laboratory animals, it is clear that animals who are dependent on cocaine will take that drug rather than food and water if they are faced with that choice. And they will do so even if that choice leads to their death.

It is harmful enough when a person takes only one kind of powerful illegal drug. But one of the big problems of drug abuse is that drug abusers do not take just one drug but rather several different kinds. At times, they do so because the preferred drug is not

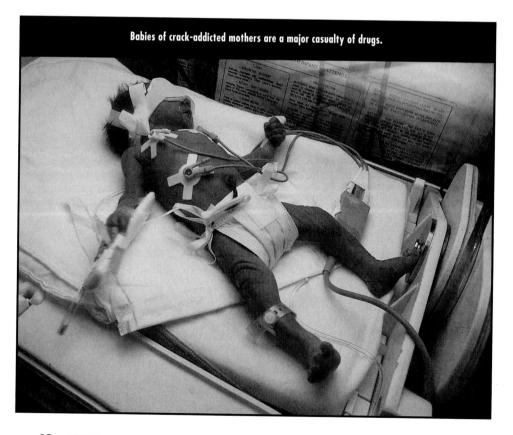

Babies of crack-addicted mothers are a major casualty of drugs.

available—often because they do not have the money to buy it. They then choose a drug that may produce a somewhat similar effect. For example, heroin addicts often turn to alcohol or tranquilizers (drugs that have a calming effect) when they cannot get heroin. It is the combination of drugs that is particularly dangerous. Barry Stimmel, Dean for Academic Affairs at The Mount Sinai School of Medicine in New York City, notes: "One 1985 study showed that 41 percent of drug-related deaths in men were related to combinations of alcohol and other drugs. Other studies show that up to 50 percent of deaths stemming from acute fatal reactions to heroin involved alcohol."

Not only do drugs damage physical and psychological health, but drug abusers may be harmed by the method of taking those drugs, as well. For example, drug addicts who inject heroin or cocaine into their blood sometimes share needles with other addicts. If an addict has AIDS and shares the needle with others who do not have AIDS, then the others will probably develop AIDS, too. About one-third of the 40,000 Americans who are infected each year with Human Immunodeficiency Virus (HIV), the virus that causes AIDS, get the disease through intravenous (within the veins) drug use. And shared needles also cause other potentially deadly illnesses, such as hepatitis, a disease of the liver.

A major casualty of drugs is not only the adult person who takes drugs but also children of pregnant women who are on drugs. For example, babies of crack-addicted mothers are often born after six months of pregnancy or earlier, rather than the normal nine months. Sometimes, they weigh as little as one to two pounds and have what has been described as "a bulb head and Popsicle limbs." At birth, the infants are already cocaine addicts. Also, drugs place a social cost on children. People who are on crack have little sense of responsibility and will do anything to get the money to feed their habit. William J. Bennett, the former drug czar, describes a Detroit woman who owed money to her drug dealer and handed over her 13-year-old daughter as payment.

Commonly Abused Drugs

Drugs may be classified as depressants or stimulants, both of which affect the central nervous system. Depressants are drugs that depress the central nervous system, resulting in the reduction of stress and excitement and a decrease in bodily activity. Depressants make users relaxed and sleepy. Narcotics are depressants and prevent a person from feeling pain. Some of the more popularly known narcotics are the opiates, such as morphine and heroin. Stimulants directly affect the central nervous system, make people feel more alert and excited, and reduce or remove tiredness. A stimulant increases the ability to stay awake and reduces fatigue. Stimulants include amphetamines, cocaine, caffeine, nicotine, and Ritalin®.

Whether using depressants or stimulants, people take drugs in a variety of ways. They snort (inhale) a drug, smoke it, inject it intravenously through a hypodermic syringe (a medical instrument used to inject fluids into a body), or eat it. How a drug is taken has an effect on how it functions in the body. When a person consumes alcohol, he or she must take it orally, which is a slow way to produce a high. When cocaine and heroin are snorted or shot into the veins, they provide a much more direct and powerful dose to the brain so that a high is produced much more quickly than in the other ways. But the fastest and most powerful way for a substance to reach the brain is by smoking, the method in which many people who use crack (an illegal substance) or tobacco (a legal substance) become addicted.

Some of the more commonly abused drugs are heroin, cocaine, marijuana, methamphetamine, and LSD. Some of these drugs come from plants, which may be processed through the use of chemicals. And some drugs are entirely synthetic.

Heroin. Heroin—sometimes called "dope" or "smack"—is a depressant. It is a powerfully addictive narcotic that comes from morphine, which itself is a product of a plant called the opium poppy. But heroin is three to five times more powerful than morphine. Heroin can be taken by smoking, snorting, injecting under the skin (skin-popping), and injecting intravenously (mainlining).

Many heroin addicts prefer to inject heroin into the muscle, under the skin, or into the veins because they enjoy the "rush," a feeling that is quick and powerful. Heroin is highly addictive. It produces an effect of extreme happiness and/or extreme depression. It often makes users sleepy. As indicated above, people who inject heroin intravenously have a good chance of developing HIV and hepatitis and risk an early death.

Cocaine. Cocaine is a stimulant that energizes its user so that he or she works harder and for longer periods. It is produced in many forms. Cocaine hydrochloride is made by processing the leaves of the coca plant into a paste at a laboratory through the use of chemicals. The paste is processed into a white crystalline powder. It is then mixed with sugar and other substances. Because of its chemical properties, cocaine hydrochloride cannot be smoked. It is used by snorting or injecting intravenously.

Crack is cocaine in a form different from cocaine hydrochloride. It is produced by chemically converting cocaine hydrochloride into a substance that can be smoked. The process is known as "freebase," and the method used to produce it has its dangers. Richard Pryor, the comedian, nearly killed himself in a freebase explosion. Crack gets its name from the cracking sound it creates both during processing and smoking. Crack, then, is smokable cocaine, costing as little as $5 a vial. It produces a quick but brief high that lasts only about 15 minutes. Smoking crack causes an immediate craving for more. People who seek crack or freebase largely out of psychological or physiological necessity are called crackheads. Crackheads need more than $1,000 a month to pay for their habit. Many of them get this money by dealing drugs or by engaging in property crimes. Women crackheads sometimes turn to prostitution to get money to pay for their drug habit. Many people addicted to crack move into crack houses, dwellings for crack addicts who live in dirty and unhealthy surroundings.

Cocaine places great stress on the human body by increasing the heart rate and breathing rate. It raises the chance for heart attack, cerebral hemorrhage (bleeding of the brain), or convulsions (abnormal muscle disturbances). A person withdrawing from cocaine becomes exhausted and depressed. Cocaine use can produce mental illness. Although it is rare, it is possible for a first-time user of cocaine to die from the drug.

Marijuana. Marijuana—sometimes called "pot" or "grass"—comes from dried leaves of the Indian hemp plant *Cannabis sativa.* Marijuana is sometimes called cannabis. One preparation made from the *Cannabis sativa* plant is known as hashish. Its use is 12,000 years old. China used it as long ago as 3000 B.C. The active ingredient of marijuana is tetrahydrocannabinol (THC). Some people classify marijuana as a stimulant, but others identify it as a depressant or hallucinogen. Of the people who use illegal drugs, more use marijuana than all other illegal drugs combined. It is often the first illegal drug that teenagers use.

Marijuana is usually smoked, but it can be eaten. Marijuana has health hazards. It interferes with short-term memory and the ability to learn and understand. It affects coordination and reduces judgment, abilities that should be unimpaired when, for example, one drives a car or handles machinery. It damages lungs and contains more cancer-causing agents than tobacco.

Methamphetamine. Methamphetamine is a synthetic drug that is also known as "speed," "crystal," "crank," and "ice." It can be swallowed, snorted, injected, or smoked. It is a member of the amphetamine family that acts as a stimulant on the central nervous system. It produces a sense of euphoria (a feeling of great happiness), with possible side effects including psychosis (severe mental disorder), paranoia (a tendency toward delusions, usually of persecution), depression, and violent behavior that can last for days. Methamphetamine was discovered in 1919. Known as "pep pills" because they keep people alert, methamphetamine became popular in the 1960s and 1970s among students, athletes, truckers, and housewives, and among "hippies" (people, usually young, who rejected conventional behavior).

Hallucinogens. Hallucinogens are mood-altering drugs that affect how people see things. The two most common hallucinogens are LSD and phencyclidine (PCP or "angel dust"). LSD is a synthetic drug that is taken orally. People under the influence of LSD, which is sometimes called "acid," experience hallucinations. In addition, LSD can cause problems with sleep and diet. Worse, it may lead to an inability to function normally in the real world. LSD was made famous by its use in the 1960s and is still used today. PCP can create a feeling of euphoria and produce violent behavior. For adolescents, PCP, like marijuana and other drugs, may harm academic performance.

Other drugs. Many drugs other than those mentioned above can also cause great physical and mental problems, and the list is enormous. Tobacco and alcohol, for example, are legal drugs, but they do more harm than all illegal drugs combined. Tobacco is the drug that causes the biggest health problems in America. It contains nicotine, a substance that causes addiction. Nicotine is even more addictive than heroin. Alcohol is responsible for up to 40 percent of general hospital admissions, and perhaps 20 percent of the nation's total expenditure for medical care.

Prescription drugs are legal, too, and can be abused. And similarly, people can cause themselves great damage by inhaling perfectly legal products, like paint, glue, nail polish remover, and propane. They do so to get a high. But inhaling items for this effect may produce headaches. Long-term use of inhalants may result in hepatitis or brain damage. Warnings on the product labels often mention the dangers.

Among the newer harmful drugs is Rohypnol, manufactured by Swiss pharmaceutical giant Hoffmann-La Roche Ltd. for treatment of severe insomnia (inability to sleep). It is sold and marketed in 80 countries, including many in Europe and South America. The manufacturer has never tried to get approval to sell it in the United States, so it is not legal to bring it into this country. Rohypnol has a strong tranquilizing effect and is seven to ten times more powerful than Valium®, a tranquilizing drug prescribed to relieve anxiety. Police believe that Rohypnol can be responsible for sexual assaults. When

SNIFFING CORRECTION FLUID CAN STOP YOUR HEART.

If you sniff to get high, you're inhaling poisons that do definite damage. So stop. Before your heart does. ⭐ Texas Prevention Partnership
1-800-269-4237

Everyday household products such as glue, paint, markers, and correction fluid are extremely dangerous
and sometimes even lethal when inhaled.

the drug is put into a victim's drink, the person who consumes it is unable to resist sexual assault and often does not even remember the attack once the individual is awake. For this reason, the media (the means of mass communications, such as newspapers, magazines, and television) describe Rohypnol as the "date-rape" drug.

Treatment

Drugs kill. They can kill quickly. A person may die from just the first experiment with a drug. Maybe this occurs because, lacking manufacturing supervision by government authorities, the drugs may contain poisonous materials. Or possibly death may result from a combination of alcohol and illegal drugs. Drugs can also kill slowly. A person may become so addicted that he or she becomes incapable of coping with life and may wind up as one of the thousands of homeless people who live in shabby, makeshift shelters, where they are subject to becoming targets of criminals. Also, a person who becomes addicted may move into a life of crime in order to obtain enough money to pay for drugs. Involvement with criminal gangs puts people who move in those circles at risk of losing their lives.

Those people who are in serious danger of addiction can get help. ("Where You Can Get More Information" on p. 123 contains a list of organizations that provide information about drug treatment.) There are a variety of treatment opportunities for people on drugs.

People do get off drugs either through their own efforts or through treatment. During the Vietnam War, for example, 15 percent of U.S. soldiers regularly used heroin and could be called addicts. Yet 90 percent of the heroin users stopped taking heroin as soon as they returned home.

One treatment is pharmacological (pertaining to the use of drugs to deal with medical problems). For opium dependence, there are two pharmacological treatments that are often used. One is long-term and involves maintaining the addict with a legally approved narcotic, such as methadone. The other treatment is detoxification in which the addict's body is cleansed of drugs.

Rehabilitation for recovering drug addicts often involves group counseling.

Outpatient drug-free treatment is a rehabilitation (restoration to a state of health) treatment in which addicts live in their own homes and make regular or occasional visits to a particular treatment source. It is a popular method that includes psychiatric treatment, counseling, and group support from recovering addicts. During inpatient treatment, individuals leave their homes and enter a facility, such as a hospital that supervises detoxification and provides psychiatric care for people with mental problems. Therapeutic communities are long-term residential treatment centers that are highly structured. They are designed for hard-core drug users who have not been successful with other treatment.

Chapter 3
THE WAR ON DRUGS

Debate: Can the War on Drugs Effectively Disrupt the Flow of Illegal Drugs into the United States?

Speaking in the White House on June 17, 1971, Richard Nixon became the first President to declare a war on drugs. "America's public enemy number one in the United States is drug abuse," he said. "In order to fight and defeat this enemy, it is necessary to wage a new, all-out offensive." And so began a war that not only Nixon, but every President since he left office, has waged.

War is a state of open conflict between countries or parties. Not only does it have a military aspect in which armed forces are used, but it has economic, social, and ideological (concerned with ideas) sides, as well. In many respects, the war on drugs follows the patterns of major conflicts in which the United States has been involved, such as World War II, the Korean War, and the Vietnam War. All of these wars were international conflicts in which American armed forces fought overseas. The drug war is international, too, although most of the armed conflict occurs within the borders of the United States and other countries and is often carried out by law-enforcement, rather than military, forces. The economic side of the drug war involves conflict over money from drug profits. The social side of the drug war centers on groups that may be attracted to taking or dealing in drugs. And the ideological side of the drug war focuses on education and

THE THRILL
CAN KILL

JUST SAY
NO
TO DRUGS

Former First Lady Nancy Reagan educated youth about the dangers of drugs with her "Just Say No" campaign in 1987.

propaganda about the effects of drugs on individuals.

The purpose of the war on drugs is to end drug use in the United States. The strategy is to reduce supply and demand. Supply reduction includes attacking production capabilities, carrying out successful interdiction (cutting off, forbidding), preventing distribution, disrupting suppliers, and breaking up finance and control systems of drug organizations. To reduce demand, U.S. government agencies with the support of private antidrug groups participate in a variety of efforts. Schools throughout the United States conduct antidrug education programs. Government agencies and private companies have drug-free workplace programs, including drug tests, to discourage drug use. (See Chapter 7.) At times, prominent public officials help publicize the dangers of drugs. As the wife of President Ronald Reagan, Nancy Reagan won much praise for her "Just Say No" antidrug educational campaign. And government at all levels has put in place increasingly severe punishments for both drug dealers and drug users.

For purposes of the following debate, the focus is on the international supply side of the issue. To be sure, the demand side is as important as the supply side because if people do not want drugs, the suppliers will have no market for their goods. But issues of the demand side are considered elsewhere in the book, most prominently in the debate on decriminalization in Chapter 4.

DEBATED:

CAN THE WAR ON DRUGS EFFECTIVELY DISRUPT THE FLOW OF ILLEGAL DRUGS INTO THE UNITED STATES?

Yes. The United States has declared a war on drugs. The people who are fighting that war can take pride in the fact that the nation is winning the contest. Winning a war of this nature, however, does not mean completely ending all sales and use of illegal drugs. It does mean that the drug problem becomes less severe over time. In fighting the war, the United States uses interdiction, international cooperation, and financial controls as its major instruments of disrupting the flow of narcotics.

Interdiction. The illegal drug business is vulnerable to detection and attack at many points. There are five stages in the chain from production to distribution: cultivation, processing, transit, wholesale distribution, and retail sale on the streets. In its efforts to deal with the international drug traffickers, the U.S. government focuses on the first three stages. And the way it fights the war depends on the nature of the drug that is being imported, as the examples of cocaine and methamphetamine show.

The Cali cartel, which dominates narcotics in Colombia, imports cocaine base from Peru and Bolivia. (A cartel is an alliance of independent business organizations formed to regulate production, pricing, and marketing of goods by its members.) The Cali cartel converts the cocaine base into cocaine powder at its laboratories in Colombia. It then smuggles the cocaine powder to the United States by air, sea, and land. Most of the cocaine is first sent to a transit country, usually Mexico. (A drug transit country is a country in which drugs pass through on their way to countries in which those drugs are distributed.) The cocaine is then shipped directly to distribution centers, including New York, Miami, New Orleans, Houston,

Phoenix, and Los Angeles and indirectly to Chicago, Philadelphia, and San Francisco. The distribution centers transport it elsewhere in the United States. Eventually it is distributed by dealers to users.

Producers of synthetic drugs like methamphetamine do not require drug crops like coca or opium for manufacturing the drugs. Instead, they need easily obtainable chemicals. The path from supplier to user of methamphetamine, or speed, is different from the path from supplier to user of cocaine. Countries that produce ephedrine, a substance used in making methamphetamine, are scattered throughout the world and include China, India, the Czech Republic, Germany, and United Arab Emirates. Some ephedrine is shipped to Mexico, sometimes through Switzerland or Guatemala, and then smuggled into the United States, although both Mexico and the United States process ephedrine. The United States also produces ephedrine and ships it directly to laboratories within its borders. Some ephedrine is channeled to middlemen. These are traders who buy from producers and sell to retailers or consumers in other transit countries. Drug cartels distribute the methamphetamine through their drug-dealing outlets.

Because the drug chain from the production of plants and raw materials to street distribution is so vast, it offers many targets for law-enforcement officials to destroy or disrupt. Law-enforcement officials well understand the importance of interdiction. First, it reduces the amount of illegal drugs coming into the United States. Second, it disrupts the production and distribution

Table 3.1

Major Drug-Producing and Drug-Transit Countries			
Argentina	Colombia	Jamaica	Paraguay
The Bahamas	Dominican Republic	Laos	Peru
Belize	Ecuador	Lebanon	Syria
Bolivia	Guatemala	Malaysia	Taiwan
Brazil	Haiti	Mexico	Thailand
Burma (Myanmar)	Hong Kong	Nigeria	Venezuela
Cambodia	India	Pakistan	Vietnam
China	Iran	Panama	

Source: U.S. Department of State. Bureau of International Narcotics and Law Enforcement Affairs. *International Narcotics Control Strategy Report: March 1996.* Washington, D.C.: Government Printing Office, 1996, p. 37.

pipeline of drug traffickers. Third, it makes drugs more expensive, resulting in lower profits for the traffickers and higher costs to would-be consumers.

The United States uses a variety of means to prevent drugs from entering the country. Its armed forces report suspicious movement of drug carriers by air, sea, and land. Customs officials inspect individuals and cargo entering the country. The Border Patrol guards the nation's borders and also plays a role in stopping drug runners.

The United States has been able to disrupt trafficking patterns of the drug trade. According to ONDCP, a third of the cocaine produced in South America is intercepted before it hits U.S. streets or those of other countries. One highly effective interdiction program, "Operation Green Clover," took place in 1995. In that effort, the U.S. military provided radar data to the Peruvian and Colombian armies that allowed them to shoot or force down trafficker aircraft. This practice disrupted the link between the coca-growing areas of Peru and the processing labs of Colombia. An aide to drug czar Barry R. McCaffrey described the operation as "the most significant disruption of the cocaine trade in 30 years." So long as traffickers face this kind of disruption, they cannot be sure that they can get their illegal drugs into the United States. They have to devote more and more resources to finding new sources of plants or chemicals to make their illicit products. They have to worry that they will require replacements for the traffickers who are arrested by law-enforcement officials.

It is true that drug traffickers look for and find new means of bringing in drugs after old paths have been disrupted. We should not feel a sense of defeatism when this happens, however, because even modest success is still success. If there were no interdiction, drug traffickers would bring even more drugs into the United States than they do now. These drugs would increase the supply and reduce the price of drugs, resulting in even more damage to Americans as well as disruption of our treatment and rehabilitation efforts. Interdiction works and saves lives for which we have to be grateful.

International cooperation. The United States provides assistance to countries that are either producers of plants, such as coca, opium poppies, and marijuana; manufacturers of illegal drugs; or transit regions in which drugs are first shipped before they are taken into the United States. (See Table 3.1.) The assistance has taken the form of providing equipment, training, law-enforcement help, and drug eradication (destruction). The United States has negotiated treaties with individual countries to allow it to try drug dealers who live in those countries. It has also worked with international organizations in all aspects of fighting drug trafficking.

Many U.S. agencies work closely with foreign countries to deal with drug trafficking. The DEA, for example, maintains 70 offices in 49 countries worldwide as part of carrying out U.S. international drug strategy. The United States gives helicopters and technical assistance to countries for use by foreign military and police personnel in their efforts to destroy narcotics and drug-manufacturing laboratories. It trains foreign investigators and judges so that they may more effectively deal with traffickers through modern means of law enforcement. For example, it helped set up special counternarcotics units in Bolivia and Peru in 1983 and trained the people who staffed those units. And in 1994, the Department of State funded antinarcotics law-enforcement training programs for foreign personnel from more than 70 countries.

The United States has supported programs in foreign countries to go after the sources of drugs by offering help in getting farmers who produce crops, such as coca, opium, and marijuana, to substitute other crops that cannot be used in making drugs. In 1971, for example, the Nixon administration succeeded in getting Turkey to destroy its opium crop by agreeing to pay Turkey for losses resulting from reduced poppy cultivation. Today, AID, which is concerned with promoting economic development, provides economic assistance and employment grants for countries to help offset the losses resulting from reducing drug exports.

The United States also supports the policy of producer countries that are willing to use chemical herbicides (plant killers) to destroy crops that can be used to make narcotics. Many countries that produced drug plants resisted the eradication programs at first but now participate in them. In 1996, for example, Peru issued a decree initiating a limited coca eradication program. And in 1995, Bolivia removed 5,500 hectares (13,590 acres) of mature, fully productive coca.

Law enforcement has offered other opportunities for the United States. When drug traffickers are arrested in a foreign country, they are usually brought to trial in that country. But the United States has had some success in bringing some of those traffickers to justice in U.S. courts because it has extradition treaties with some countries. Extradition is a method by which one country sends an accused criminal to another country that has the legal authority to try that individual. Under an extradition treaty, drug traffickers who live in a drug-producing country and receive indictments (statements of criminal charges) in a U.S. court can be sent from that country to the United States for prosecution. For example, Colombia extradited drug lord Carlos Lehder Rivas to the United States where he faced a trial. In 1988, he was convicted of smuggling three tons of cocaine into the United States.

In 1995, Pakistan extradited three leading heroin traffickers to the United States. That same year, Thailand began extradition proceedings against ten major drug traffickers. Drug traffickers in drug-producing and drug-transit countries usually prefer to be tried in their own countries, because some of them can either bribe judges and jurors to get a favorable verdict or serve more lenient sentences than they would if convicted and imprisoned in the United States.

In part because of U.S. pressure, foreign governments themselves are getting more serious about trying and convicting drug traffickers in their own courts. According to a U.S. State Department report: "By early 1996, there were more prominent drug figures behind bars than in any comparable period in the past few years."

The United States seeks to use economic pressure to persuade countries that produce or distribute narcotics to become effective in stopping the flow of narcotics into the United States. One of the means for exerting that pressure has been established through the use of the certification process. Under the law, the President is required to certify (assure) that all drug-producing or drug-transit countries are "cooperating fully" with U.S. antidrug policies or have taken their own measures against drugs and financial wrongdoing with drug money. Those countries not certified receive sanctions (penalties) in that they are shut off from most types of U.S. assistance. In addition, the United States votes against them in their efforts to obtain loans from certain international banks. The law does allow for some flexibility, however. If a country does not comply with the policy, the law allows the President to issue a waiver (the intentional giving up of a right, claim, or privilege) based on the national security interests of the United States. But even a country that receives a waiver becomes the subject of condemnation by the international community and fears that one day it will lose its certification.

Although the denial of certification carries economic sanctions, the countries affected often are more concerned about their reputation for not living up to the standard set by the law. As the State Department annual report on certification in 1996 notes: "The last thing any government wants impugned [criticized] before its international peers [equals] is its honor or integrity, especially when it must publicly confront objective, if often damaging evidence that it has not cooperated fully in countering the drug trade."

Critics of certification say that the United States does not apply the same standards in choosing which countries it certifies. It continues to certify Mexico, a major transit country for drugs, for example, but it withdrew certification from Colombia, a major drug-producing country. But the Mexican government has made a sincere commitment to the struggle against drugs.

Mexico is under heavy assault by the international drug cartels and is fighting back. Mexico deserves U.S. support.

Certification, whatever its limitations, remains an influential weapon in the war on drugs. Most of the countries that receive waivers or are denied certification begin to take steps against drug trafficking. After the United States made certification decisions in 1995, Nigeria and Pakistan arrested some drug traffickers and extradited them to the United States, Bolivia began a crop eradication campaign again, and Peru took measures against drug flights, according to ONDCP. As of 1996, the countries denied certification were Afghanistan, Burma, Colombia, Iran, Nigeria, and Syria. Countries with vital national security interest certifications are Lebanon, Pakistan, and Paraguay.

Finally, the United States has worked with international organizations to fight drug trafficking. It has, for example, worked to strengthen the efforts to control precursor chemicals. (See Table 3.2.) Article 12 of the 1988 United Nations Convention Against Illicit Traffic in Narcotic Drugs and Psychotropic Substances (1988 UN Convention) establishes the obligation for parties to the treaty to control their chemical commerce to prevent diversion to illicit drug manufacture. The annexes (additions) to the Convention list 22 chemicals as those most necessary to drug manufacture, and therefore subject to control. These chemicals come from many countries and are used not only for purposes of manufacturing illegal drugs but for legitimate industrial purposes, as well. For example, widely used industrial chemicals, such as sulfuric acid and acetic anhydride, are used to refine the coca leaf into cocaine and crack, and opium into morphine and heroin. So the illegal use of these chemicals for drug manufacturing is difficult to track.

Table 3.2

Major Precursor Chemical Source Countries
Argentina
Brazil
China
Germany
India
Mexico
The Netherlands

Source: U.S. Department of State, Bureau of International Narcotics and Law Enforcement Affairs. *International Narcotics Control Strategy Report: March 1996.* Washington, D.C.: Government Printing Office, 1996, p. 37.

Most major chemical and drug-producing countries now have chemical control laws and regulations in place to meet the chemical control obligations of the 1988 UN Convention. And the United States points to effective steps that are being taken by other countries to control precursor chemicals. For example, in the summer of 1995, before India placed strict controls on precursor chemicals, a ton of ephedrine could be purchased on the black market for approximately $54,000. But in December of that year, the same amount of ephedrine was demanding a price of approximately $80,000. The State Department observes that the rise in prices and reduction in availability of precursor chemicals come about in part because of strong enforcement efforts.

Financial controls. The amount of money involved in the drug trade is astounding, although estimates differ about the exact figure. The United Nations Commission on Narcotic Drugs calculates the global trade in illegal drugs as a $500 billion-a-year industry. The International Criminal Police Organization (Interpol) sets the figure at $400 billion. Even if it is the lower figure, this amount is higher than the gross domestic product (a nation's total output of goods and services) of all but the wealthiest countries.

Because illegal drugs involve so much money, dealers have a problem with tax authorities who hope to trace the funds. Obviously, the dealers accept cash only in an effort to prevent the government from obtaining evidence that can be used to arrest and convict them. In their attempt to avoid detection, they engage in money laundering. U.S. law-enforcement agencies estimate that between $100 billion and $300 billion in U.S. currency is laundered every year. Drug dealers have found many ways to launder money. For example, they deposit small amounts of money in a bank and then send it off to an account in a foreign bank. Or they buy or control a bank and secretly move funds through bank channels. Modern electronic means of sending money to any place in the world in seconds simplifies their efforts to get away with their crimes.

Table 3.3

Major Money-Laundering Countries		
Argentina	Japan	Spain
Aruba	Liechtenstein	Switzerland
Brazil	Luxembourg	Thailand
Canada	Mexico	Turkey
Cayman Islands	The Netherlands	United Arab Emirates
Colombia	Netherland Antilles	United Kingdom
Costa Rica	Nigeria	United States
Ecuador	Pakistan	Switzerland
Germany	Panama	Uruguay
Hong Kong	Paraguay	Venezuela
India	Russia	
Italy	Singapore	

Source: U.S. Department of State. Bureau of International Narcotics and Law Enforcement Affairs. *International Narcotics Control Strategy Report:*
March 1996. Washington, D.C.: Government Printing Office, 1996, p. 37.

Still, drug dealers are vulnerable. They have to worry not only about losing just tax money but losing all of the money they gained from drug trafficking, as well. In 1986, Congress enacted a strong law against money laundering and made it easy to confiscate (seize by the government for the public treasury) money and property obtained as a result of the sale of illegal drugs. The United States has been increasingly successful in getting countries to go after money-laundering activities. (See Table 3.3.) More than 100 countries have ratified (approved) the 1988 Convention, which among other goals seeks to hit the financial resources of drug traffickers. Many of these nations have passed laws of their own to curb money laundering.

Governments have weapons to attack money laundering. Drug profits must go through international banking channels that are subject to government supervision. Also, the amount of money in drug trafficking is so high that it is difficult to conceal in the banking system. Moreover, the United States and other governments have taken steps to find the drug money and remove it from the hands of drug traffickers and distributors.

On October 22, 1995, President Bill Clinton delivered a speech at the United Nations in which he announced a new U.S. effort against money laundering. A few days later, he issued Presidential Decision Directive 42 that deals with money laundering. It directs government agencies to identify the biggest drug traffickers, their associates, and companies they have set up and freeze—make unavailable—their assets in the United States. After identifying the drug violators, the directive states, "the Secretary of the Treasury can prohibit any U.S. person from engaging in financial transactions or trade with those identified individuals or enterprises." The United States acted against 80 designated individuals and businesses found to be significant foreign narcotics traffickers, including those who assist in laundering trafficker proceeds through financial transactions. The order blocked

President Bill Clinton announces the new U. S. effort against money laundering to the United Nations.

the assets in the United States and U.S. banks overseas of these traffickers, and the individuals and companies doing business on their behalf. The Treasury Department published a list of the companies and individuals and notified U.S. companies and banks to block their assets and prohibit trade with them.

It is easy to be cynical and defeatist about the war on drugs. Perhaps there is much wisdom in the view of General McCaffrey that the term "war" is inappropriate for the effort to fight drugs. He prefers to think of the drug problem as a potentially deadly but treatable disease, which requires long and continuing struggles. Fighting this disease will take much patience against seemingly impossible conditions. But the stakes are too high to give in to the voices of despair and defeat. Even the most committed of government antidrug law-enforcement officials understand that the United States is not stopping drugs from coming into the United States. But what they correctly recognize is that drug traffickers will be even more successful if the United States makes no efforts to control the drug supply. Drugs would then become even cheaper on the market, resulting in their greater use. The police in the United States would then face an impossible task of being the only obstacles for drug traffickers to overcome.

NO. For nearly three decades, Presidents and other public officials have announced that they were leading the country into a war on drugs. And so they have. But that war is costly and shows no signs of victory. It is clear that the United States cannot win that war, at least in terms of disrupting the flow of illegal substances into the country.

Interdiction. Law-enforcement officials seize planes and boats containing illegal drugs, and they are careful to publicize their successes in the media. But the flow of drugs remains constant. The most optimistic accounts show that law-enforcement officials are successful in stopping only 10 percent of the illegal drugs coming into the country. And it is not surprising why this is so. The United States cannot control its borders, and it cannot find the illegal drugs coming into the country because the movement of people and goods into the country is so enormous.

When law-enforcement officials seal one border, the drug smugglers find other ways of getting through. For example, in an attempt to stop marijuana from coming into the United States, U.S. border officials on September 21, 1969 set in motion Operation Intercept in which they stopped every vehicle crossing the border from Mexico heading for the United States. Mexicans complained about the long delays in border crossings, and the operation ended after twenty days. A consequence of Operation Intercept was a considerable increase in the number of aircraft flying drugs illegally across the border.

Even the much-praised Operation Green Clover was a temporary success for the U.S. antidrug effort. Traffickers found other routes through rivers and moved air and ground traffic elsewhere. According to the State Department's report on the international narcotics trade, Peru actually increased its cultivation and production of coca in 1995.

It is no wonder that smugglers get their merchandise into the country, given America's huge borders. The United States has a 1,933-mile (3,110-km) border with Mexico and two borders with Canada that equal 5,525 miles (8,890 km). It has a coastline of 12,385 miles (19,930 km). Smugglers use many techniques

During Operation Intercept in 1969, border officials stopped every vehicle crossing the border from Mexico into the United States.

to bring in drugs. Illegal drugs come in by plane or boat. Drug runners carry their illegal shipments with them as they walk or drive across the Mexican-U.S. border illegally. Given the vast amount of imports into the United States, smugglers put illegal drugs into legitimate cargo containers. Sometimes, they hide them in seemingly innocent products, such as automobile tires. Just two automobile tires being exported from a foreign country to the United States could be filled with enough heroin to be worth $10 million. Smugglers have hidden drugs in the coffins of dead people whose bodies were transported to the United States. And just before boarding a flight to the United States, some smugglers swallow cocaine in balloons. If the balloons burst while in the body, the smugglers may die. For some smugglers, however, the rewards are worth the risk. About half a million people enter the United States legally each year. It is impossible to check thoroughly all the incoming people and their possessions. And U.S. Customs officials say that only 3 percent of the 9 million containers that enter the United States by sea each year are inspected by customs inspectors.

The Office of Technology Assessment (OTA), a former agency of Congress, noted in 1987 that despite a doubling of federal expenditures on interdiction in the previous five years, "the quantity of drugs is greater than ever...." The OTA concluded: "There is no clear correlation [connection] between the level of expenditures or effort devoted to interdiction and the long-term availability of illegally imported drugs in the domestic market."

Law-enforcement officials take great pride in showing their successes at interdicting drugs. And they do have successes. Cocaine seizure totals increased from 1989 to 1992, for example. But cocaine availability appears to have increased in that period, too.

Even if the United States seals its borders, it cannot shut itself off from drugs. If, for example, the United States stopped all marijuana from entering the country, it could still produce enough in the United States itself. It has been estimated that up to 25 percent of the marijuana consumed in the United States is domestically grown already. The market would be bigger except that it is cheaper to produce marijuana in Mexico than it is in the United States. If coca leaves and opium poppies were stopped from coming into the United States from foreign countries, there are enough places in the United States that are suitable for growing these plants, too. Also, laboratories in the United States could (and do) produce synthetic drugs. The war on drugs would not end if foreign imports were cut off.

International cooperation. U.S. efforts to gain the cooperation of other nations have not been effective in reducing the flow of drugs into the United States. One important reason why the United States cannot stop or sharply reduce the drug flow is because it has only a limited ability to influence other countries. The United States lives in a world of independent countries. It needs the cooperation of other countries not only in its drug policy but in other policies, as well. When U.S. officials feel that these other policies are more important than U.S. drug policies, then, however reluctantly, U.S. officials are willing to downplay the war on drugs.

An example of the conflict between drug and other policies occurred in the decades following World War II, when the major issue of U.S. foreign policy was winning the "cold war" with the Soviet Union and other Communist countries. The cold war is the term that is used to indicate the continuing conflict between the two countries along economic, political, and ideological lines, which lasted for nearly a half century. It also involved for each of these countries the creation of a military force strong enough to deter an armed attack by the opposing side. It is a cold war and not a hot war because the conflict does not break down into an actual direct clash of opposing armed forces.

In its effort to challenge the Soviet Union and other countries that supported the ideas of communism that the Soviet Union championed, the United States sought alliances with governments and private groups that were anticommunist. In some cases, these groups were involved in international drug trafficking. Some of the drugs handled by these traffickers found their way into cities and towns in the United States. In other words, the United States was supporting drug suppliers at the same time that it was denouncing the evil drug trade.

The CIA has had a long history of minimizing the importance of drugs, giving its major attention to the cold war. There is reason to believe, for example, that in the 1950s a CIA-supported Chinese army fought the Communist Chinese but at the same time engaged in drug trafficking. In the 1960s, the CIA aided tribesmen in Laos, who were also drug traffickers. Similarly, when the Soviet Union was fighting Afghanistan in the 1980s, the U.S. supported Afghan rebels and Pakistanis who were involved in the drug trade.

Although vital national interests limit the ability of the United States to influence friendly countries, there are other restrictions on the power of the United States to force or influence a country to aid U.S. efforts in the war on drugs. Foremost perhaps of these other restrictions is the role of national honor that is felt by the people of many countries. The people of a foreign country enlisted in the war on drugs may ask: "By what right do you in the United States tell us what to do?" And, "What would you think if we sent our armed forces or law-enforcement officials into your country to get your law-enforcement officials to solve our problems?" Many Latin American countries in particular experienced U.S. military intervention and in some cases even occupation in the 19th and 20th centuries. Some people in those countries regard U.S. antidrug war efforts as just another form of imperialism—the policy of a strong nation using its power to dominate a weak nation—and they resent American interventionism of any kind in their country.

Even when foreign countries agree to go along with U.S. drug policies, they often fail for lack of resources or political will, or both. When they succeed, the results are often temporary gains. For example, although the United

States has had some successes in getting farmers to substitute legal products for the drug products that they plant, for the most part, the substitution policy has failed. Coca is a case in point. Poor peasants in Bolivia and Peru are struggling to survive financially. No other crop in Bolivia brings in as much money to the farmers as coca. When farmers grow coca crops, the drug traffickers pay them money immediately upon delivery. Even if the government of Bolivia or Peru agrees to work with the United States to destroy the coca crops, the price of the crops rises and, thus, coca becomes even more tempting for farmers to produce. The United States has not been able to defeat the coca producers. When law-enforcement officials destroy their crops, the farmers plant elsewhere. They hide crops and relocate drug laboratories. When necessary, coca growers have resorted to strikes, blockades, and even armed resistance to carry on their work.

But even if the United States were successful in destroying coca leaves or in getting the Andean peasants (those from the region of the Andes Mountains in South America) to stop producing them, the effect on cocaine use in the United States would be small. It would not affect the street price and force a lowering of demand because of price pressures, for example. Economist Peter Reuter calculates that a reduction of 50 percent in the Andean supply (an amount that is regarded as impossibly high to achieve) would have only a small influence on the street price of drugs because the largest part of the price of drugs is added on after the drugs get to the United States.

Let us imagine, though, that the United States were successful in stopping drug growing and production in one country; it could not achieve the same effect worldwide. The drug trade operates in what is known as the "balloon principle": When a finger is pressed at one point on a balloon, that point collapses, but the balloon expands at another point. The total volume remains the same. For example, in 1971, the Nixon administration succeeded in getting Turkey to destroy its opium crop by agreeing to pay Turkey for losses resulting from reduced poppy cultivation. And heroin from Turkey stopped being a principal source of that substance in the early 1970s. The Turkish ban on opium in 1972 and the smashing of a French drug ring led to a search for supplies elsewhere. According to the DEA, by 1974, Mexican traffickers controlled three-quarters of the U.S. heroin market. Burma, Thailand, and Laos—countries in Southeast Asia known as the Golden Triangle—soon became a supplier of opium. Then, Afghanistan, Pakistan, and Iran—known as the Golden Crescent—became an opium center.

According to the U.S. State Department's *International Narcotics Control Strategy Report* in 1996, there are 31 countries that are either major producers of drugs or are staging areas through which drugs transit. Fifteen of these countries are in South America or the Caribbean, 12 are in Asia or the Indian Subcontinent, three are in the Middle East, and one is in Africa. In addition, the State Department reports that seven countries produce chemicals used in the manufacture or refining of illegal drugs, and 33 countries are major money-laundering countries and territories. There are plenty of opportunities for drug traffickers to switch locations when law-enforcement becomes threatening.

Trying to stop heroin imports by attacking them at the source must be a failure. According to drug expert David F. Musto, U.S. heroin demand can be met by the amount of opium poppies growing on a 10- to 20-square mile (26- to 52-km^2) patch of land. Given such a small requirement of land, it is unrealistic to suppose that attacking heroin in any one country will do much good to halt supply. Nor is the story different for cocaine. It is estimated that the annual cocaine needs of the United States could fit in 13 trailer trucks.

U.S. efforts at encouraging eradication programs have sometimes damaged more than drug crops. Steven B. Duke and Albert C. Gross report in their book *America's Longest War: Rethinking Our Tragic Crusade Against Drugs* that according to peasants in the Cuilco valley in Guatemala, an American-sponsored herbicide program targeting opium poppies in the valley damaged part of the tomato crop and killed the bees that produced commercial honey and pollinated all other crops in the valley. Destroying legal crops cannot benefit U.S. prestige in the world.

The United States also has some responsibility for creating environmental hazards as a result of its war on drugs. Spraying pesticides causes environmental damage indirectly by creating political conditions that encourage deforestation—the clearing away of forests. Environmentalists believe that deforestation is a cause of global warming—the warming of the Earth's atmosphere by the release of carbon dioxide and other gases. This is a process that can cause great damage to the planet. The drug war contributes to deforestation by encouraging producers of coca to seek out new areas in the jungle to plant their coca. According to South American researcher Roberto Lerner, "[A]t least 10% of the [rain-forest] deforestation has been caused by coca growing and coca expansion."

The extradition treaties, too, have had a limited effect in stopping drug trafficking, as the experience of Colombia shows. Colombia and the United States signed an extradition treaty in 1979. According to the treaty, Colombia would send fugitives from American indictments for certain crimes, including drug trafficking, to the United States, where they would be tried. In 1984, Colombia extradited 16 people, including Carlos Lehder Rivas, who led the drug cartel in Medellín, a city in west central Colombia.

In 1985, guerrillas thought to be in the pay of drug lords assassinated 11 of the 24 justices of the Colombian Supreme Court along with 100 court employees. Hundreds of Colombian judges gave up their jobs for fear that they would suffer the same fate. In 1987, the Colombian Supreme Court declared the extradition treaty to be unconstitutional.

The Colombian government cracked down on the drug lords after 1989, when the government reinstated the extradition treaty with the United States. The Colombian government also arrested thousands of suspected members of drug organizations, seized property of drug lords, and extradited some drug lords to the United States. But in 1991, the government made a deal with the drug lords in which it got rid of the extradition treaty. In return drug lord Pablo Escobar and several people in his Medellín organization agreed to enter a specially built luxury prison in Colombia. But they escaped in 1992. The result was that their power over drugs did not end but was replaced to a considerable degree by the Cali cartel, which was even willing to use harsher criminal methods than the Medellín cartel. In the words of the U.S. State Department's *International Narcotics Control Strategy Report* of March 1996:

In retaliation to the extradition of drug traffickers to the United States, 11 Justices of the Colombian Supreme Court were assassinated in 1985.

"[T]hey [the international drug trafficking organizations] showed that often, far from crippling an organization, the arrest of a drug baron may only create a temporary job opening."

In December 1996, Colombian police raided La Picota Prison in Bogota, a maximum-security prison holding Miguel and Bulberto Rodriguez Orejudela and most of the other leaders of the Cali cartel. Most of the leaders of the Cali cartel had been arrested or surrendered in 1995 on minor drug-trafficking charges. In return, they received sentences of less than ten years. But the prison facilities with which they were provided were not like those for other criminals but were rather a setting for a life of great comfort. In prison, the drug lords had the protection of their bodyguards and were allowed many visitors. They used the prison phone and their meetings with their visitors to continue to run their drug business. Law-enforcement authorities tapped the phone and discovered that the traffickers were trying to arrange for the bribery of key Colombian legislators.

The ability of the United States to persuade foreign countries to fight the drug war has not been strengthened by U.S. certification policy because the United States cannot apply its certification policies in a consistent manner. In this regard the United States decertifies some countries that engage in drug trafficking but certifies other countries that have similar drug practices. This selective approach depends on the importance of a country to the national security and economic interests of the United States. For example, Burma (Myanmar) and Afghanistan are of limited national security or economic interest to the United States, and they are on the decertification list. In contrast, although Panama was heavily involved in the drug business, the United States certified it because it was supporting the U.S. policy of aiding anticommunist guerrilla groups in the war in Nicaragua. But when Panama's leader Manuel Noriega was involved in drug trafficking and became friendly to the Communist governments of Cuba and the Soviet Union, the United States turned against him and invaded Panama in 1989.

In addition, the United States refused to put Mexico on the decertification list in the 1990s, in spite of clear evidence that Mexico was a major stopping-off point for planes carrying illegal drugs from South America to the United States. By 1990, 70 percent of all the cocaine smuggled into the United States was coming in through Mexico. But U.S. trade interests with Mexico were of greater importance than the war on drugs in the making of U.S. foreign policy.

U.S. influence in drug-producing and drug-trafficking countries is limited because of the enormous power of foreign drug interests in their own countries. At times, the drug cartel controls the government, as the case of Colombia shows. Colombia is sometimes called a narco-democracy because it has the familiar trappings of democracy, such as elections, but narcotics traffickers actually dominate the political system. They use bribes to elected officials, judges, and prosecutors to influence government. And when they still cannot persuade government officials to their way of thinking, they rely on assassinations and other acts of terrorism.

The efforts of international drug-fighting organizations to affect the drug trade in any significant fashion is limited. It is so easy to get around some

U.S. troops invading Panama in 1989

of the international regulations. For example, precursor chemicals are difficult to track because they are used for many legitimate purposes. Chemical companies can secretly divert chemicals to manufacturers of illegal drugs. The countries to which the chemicals are sent may not investigate the diversion of those chemicals once they are legitimately brought into the country. Or chemicals may be shipped to a non-drug-producing country and then smuggled into a drug-producing country by being transported across borders that are largely unguarded.

Financial controls. Money laundering is difficult to monitor because there are millions of bank transactions every day. Drug dealers know how to fool tax investigators. Some drug organizations buy up banks and then use the banks as a way to recycle the drug money. Still others purchase legitimate businesses and change the account books to mislead tax authorities. Some carry the money out of the United States and deposit the money in an unlisted account of a foreign bank. The Bahamas, Cayman Islands, and Panama are among the many foreign locations where drug dealers launder their money.

Once drug dealers send their money to a foreign location in which U.S. investigators have difficulty tracing, they can draw checks or send wire transfers from their account there to people in the United States. The receivers of those funds now can show legitimate income from a foreign source. Also, the money in the tax havens can be sent to drug suppliers overseas. In this way, U.S. tax authorities are not even involved. These processes can continue so long as there is a market for illegal drugs.

Although 100 governments have ratified the 1988 UN Convention, eight governments ranked as high, medium-high, or medium priority money-laundering concerns by the U.S. government have signed but not ratified the 1988 UN Convention, and three other governments ranked among the higher priorities have not even signed. Usually, the signing of a treaty by representatives of a government marks an intent to ratify. But signature of a treaty does not create a legal obligation to live up to its terms. Ratification of a treaty, however, creates a legal obligation to do so. According to the U.S. State Department, "Thus, almost one-fifth of the 67 governments in the three highest priority categories have not ratified this universal accord six years after its declaration." And many governments adopt only weak measures against money laundering.

It is true that sometimes U.S. law-enforcement officials come up with successes and are able to get at some of the drug proceeds through forfeiture proceedings (a process in which money or property is surrendered). But forfeitures do not account for a significant disruption of the drug trade. According to Steven B. Duke and Albert C. Gross: "Forfeitures represent less than 2 percent of America's illegal drug market."

Winning the war on drugs through the attempt to effectively disrupt the flow of drugs cannot succeed. But it is not impossible to solve the problem of drug abuse. Drug use will decline when people become convinced that taking drugs is bad for them, as tobacco use declined when millions of Americans became convinced about the dangers of tobacco. Similarly, the decline of marijuana and cocaine use started before the toughening of the drug war in 1986 when people became aware of the consequences of drug use to life and health. Publicity and education will not assure that drugs fade away, but they will produce far better results than can be achieved by continuing the international war on smuggling drugs into the United States.

Chapter 4

THE DECRIMINALIZATION OF DRUGS

Debate: Should the United States Decriminalize Drugs?

A car moves into an urban area known for its drug sales. The driver is looking for someone to sell him crack. He has been to this area before and knows what to expect. Once the sale is made, he will push his foot down on the gas pedal and head to his own neighborhood where he will join his friends at a party. It has always been so easy, like buying a newspaper from a salesperson at a stop signal at a highway approach. The driver makes a purchase of drugs from a person he believes to be a drug dealer. Suddenly police vehicles circle the car, and the "dealer," who is really a police officer dressed in ordinary street clothes, yells, "I am a police officer. You are under arrest. Get out of the car." The police officer handcuffs the driver, informs him of his rights, puts him in the back of a police car, and hauls him off to the police station.

The driver is now a suspect for committing a crime. He has never been arrested before and is totally unprepared for dealing with life in the criminal justice system. The police place him in a cell with suspects for other crimes. The police permit him to call an attorney and tell him that if he cannot afford to hire one, the state will provide him with a public defender whom the state will pay to handle his defense. After several hours, he appears before a judge who decides to release him on bail. Bail is usually a sum of money given by, or on behalf of, an arrested person in exchange for his or her temporary release as security for that person's required appearance in court. The money is a guarantee that a person will appear at trial. If the person does not appear, then he or she (or the person who puts up the bail) loses that money. The police then attempt to find and arrest that person again so that they may pursue criminal proceedings in court.

Our drug purchasing suspect pays the bail and is released. He needs to return for trial in several weeks. In this case, the suspect pleads guilty and in return is required to pay a fine and agree to enter a drug-rehabilitation and testing program because this incident is a first offense. If he goes back to buying drugs, the judge rules, he will serve time in jail.

Situations such as this are not uncommon throughout the United States. Similarly, many people are arrested for possessing, using, or selling drugs. The penalty depends on many factors, including the type and amount of drugs in one's possession and the number of previous drug offenses. As this case shows, some drug-law offenders get limited sentences. But some drug dealers get lifetime sentences.

Many federal and state laws deal with the use and distribution of drugs. As mentioned in Chapter 2, some drugs, such as heroin, cocaine, and marijuana, are Schedule I drugs, and their users and distributors are subject to severe federal punishment. But state laws differ in punishment for the same drug crime. In some states, for example, the possession of marijuana is regarded as a misdemeanor (an offense of less seriousness than a major crime). A person possessing marijuana in those states is still subject to the criminal law. But the punishment may be payment of a small fine. In other states, the same crime may result in a heavy jail sentence.

Some people, particularly in law enforcement, believe that strong antidrug laws are needed to keep drug use low. But others argue that the entire approach to drugs as a crime is wrong. They favor either legalization or decriminalization. Legalization of drugs is the elimination of laws that make it a crime to use or sell drugs.

Decriminalization is the reduction of penalties for the use of drugs. With decriminalization, the drug laws remain on the books, but they apply more severely to a small category of offenders, such as big-time dealers, and provide for a less severe punishment for someone who uses drugs rather than sells them.

Most people who argue against drug laws support decriminalization rather than legalization. And most advocates of decriminalization would still make a distinction between the sale of drugs to adults and the sale of drugs to children. The latter case would still be subject to severe penalties, as is already so with the sale of alcohol to minors. Many supporters of decriminalization oppose drug use. But they believe that the drug laws do more harm than good, and they say that a person who takes drugs needs treatment rather than punishment as a criminal. In recent years, supporters of decriminalization include some well-known people in public life. Among these are conservative writer William F. Buckley, Jr., former Secretary of State George Shultz, Baltimore Mayor Kurt Schmoke, and New York District Judge Robert Sweet. But they and other advocates of decriminalization have faced strong opposition, particularly from law-enforcement officials and some professors who have studied the drug issue. Among major critics of decriminalization are former drug czar William J. Bennett, political scientist James Q. Wilson, and Joseph Califano, president of the National Center on Addiction and Substance Abuse at Columbia University. On the issue of decriminalization, there is no "liberal" or "conservative" position. Liberals are divided on the issue of decriminalization, as are conservatives.

DEBATED:

SHOULD THE UNITED STATES DECRIMINALIZE DRUGS?

Yes. The taking of illegal drugs, such as heroin, cocaine, methamphetamine, and PCP, is dangerous, and anyone who "does drugs" is not only foolish but is dumb because the consequences to life and mind are so devastating. As bad as drugs are, however, the drug laws themselves produce harmful consequences to life and mind that are even worse than the drugs themselves. Decriminalization of drugs is necessary because drug laws (1) do not reduce the demand for drugs, (2) result in high crime rates, (3) produce harmful consequences to society, and (4) ignore superior alternative methods of dealing with the drug problem.

But before explaining these arguments, let us be clear about the meaning of decriminalization. With the decriminalization of drugs, criminal penalties would still exist for certain drug behavior, such as selling drugs to kids, for example. And some kinds of behavior, such as murder or assault while under the influence of drugs, would still be considered criminal. But mere possession or use of drugs would either not be subject to criminal penalties or would be subject to minor criminal penalties.

Demand. Advocates of drug laws argue that the laws are necessary to reduce demand for drugs. But this assumption is wrong. People are more likely to reject drugs when they understand that these drugs can cause them harm rather than when they understand that these drugs are illegal. In the late 19th century, for example, scientists began to recognize the addictive nature of some drugs, particularly cocaine. At that time, a number of patent medicines contained cocaine because of a then scientific belief that cocaine had medical benefits. But scientists soon learned about the addictive nature of cocaine and publicized the danger of that substance to life and health. Companies that included cocaine in their products began to stop doing so even before Congress passed the Pure Food and Drug Act of 1906. Many people became aware of the danger and were careful to stay away from cocaine. By 1914, when federal legislation banned heroin and cocaine, the drug problem as it was then experienced had really passed. It was the knowledge of the danger of drugs that brought a decline in their use rather than laws against their use that reduced the drug threat.

According to DEA figures, the use of illegal drugs peaked in 1979 and declined in the 1980s and early 1990s. Although drug use has experienced a slight rise in recent years, it is still way below the 1979 level. But the amount of illegal drugs available for sale has not declined. If anything, it has increased. The United States is not alone in proving that drug use does not depend on drug availability. Mexico has huge amounts of drugs, but, as the U.S. State Department reports, its people do not have a serious drug problem.

In the late 19th century, a number of patent medicines contained addictive drugs such as cocaine.

Finally, even if demand increases as a result of decriminalization, the overall effect on society may still be positive. With decriminalization and proper government restrictions on the production of drugs, there will be little danger of contamination with deadly poisons that sometimes affects illegal drugs. And it is reasonable to suspect that fewer people will turn to alcohol, which is a far more dangerous drug than illegal drugs in terms of its consequences to society.

Crime. Drug laws cause crime for many reasons. First, whenever there is a demand for something, people will find a way to obtain it. Because of the demand, criminals are encouraged to enter the market as suppliers to the people who want or need drugs. The experience of the United States in attempting to end alcohol consumption is instructive.

In 1919, the nation engaged in Prohibition, which barred the sale of alcohol, as a result of the adoption of the Eighteenth Amendment to the Constitution and legislation enforcing that amendment (the Volstead Act). Prohibition was known as a "noble experiment" because those who favored the policy argued that alcoholism was a moral issue: It was responsible for destroying families and undermining traditional values. In spite of the noble purpose behind the ban, many Americans still wanted alcohol. They found illegal means to satisfy their needs. Criminals realized quickly that the market for alcohol would bring them enormous profits. They built fortunes by trafficking in illegal alcohol. Bootleggers (those who make, sell, or transport for sale alcoholic liquor illegally) found many ways to obtain and supply alcohol. Anyone who wanted to drink alcohol could do so easily by finding a speakeasy, a place that sold illegal alcohol. Prohibition not only allowed

During Prohibition, bootleggers were wanted criminals.

people who were professional criminals to find a new outlet for their crimes but turned otherwise innocent citizens into criminals merely because they sold some beer or other alcoholic drink.

Second, because the government spends so many resources in fighting the drug wars, the street cost and profits of drugs are high. The real cost of legally producing drugs is low, but criminals must add to the basic cost money spent for such illegal purposes as bribing public officials, smuggling substances into the United States, hiring lookouts to watch for police, and obtaining the best legal defense that money can buy for those drug criminals who are caught by the police. The risks of being arrested are high, thus raising the price and profits of drugs to unbelievable heights.

Estimates vary in measuring the amount of markup in heroin and cocaine. A markup is the amount added to the original cost of an item to decide its selling price. Law professor Steven B. Duke says the markup in these drugs is 5,000 percent. Other analysts place the figure at 20,000 percent. According to Joseph D. McNamara, former police chief in Kansas City, Missouri, and San Jose, California, "About $500 worth of heroin or cocaine in a source country [a country that produces it] will bring in as much as $100,000 on the streets of an American city. All the cops, armies, prisons, and executions in the world cannot impede [block] a market with that kind of tax-free profit margin."

Third, because the cost of illegal drugs is so high, thanks to the criminal character of marketing these products, people who would not otherwise be criminals turn to crime in order to get enough money to finance their habit. If the drugs are legal, however, the cost of drugs will be affordable, thus reducing the economic need for someone addicted to drugs to engage in such criminal activity. The average heroin addict needs $10,000 a year just to pay for heroin. A Bureau of Justice Statistics survey of prison inmates shows that "nearly 1 in 3 robbers and burglars said they had committed their crimes to obtain money for drugs."

Fourth, because police are so busy going after anyone doing drugs, whether small-timers or pushers, they divert their resources from focusing on serious, violent non-drug crime. The bill for fighting drugs through law enforcement is high. Steven B. Duke calculates that $347 billion is spent in fighting the war on drugs. He observes that $337 billion "was the total federal budget as recently as 1975. The crime costs of drug prohibition alone may equal 150 percent of the entire federal welfare budget for 1995." The cost of drug law enforcement makes up at least 25 percent of the nation's police budgets. In large metropolitan areas, the share of the drug law-enforcement budget is half or more. If much of the money now spent on enforcement of drug laws were spent on fighting other serious crimes, then America would be a safer place.

Fifth, decriminalization would lessen the opportunities for crime by law-enforcement officials. Judge Robert Sweet notes that one group of distributors in a case before him sold 37,500 kilograms (82,500 pounds) of cocaine a month for gross (total) sales of almost $20 million a month, and other similar groups operate in the same city as that group. With that kind of money involved in illegal drug use, it is inevitable that law-enforcement officials will engage in corruption. A former police chief in Detroit went to prison for stealing money that was supposed to be used for tempting dealers to sell drugs. Even DEA official Edward O'Brien, who helped break the French Connection case, a major drug bust, was arrested when he tried to deliver 62 pounds (28 kg) of cocaine to an informant. Police officials arrest people who are making ten times as much money as they do, so it is not surprising that some of them are on the take.

Sixth, critics of decriminalization claim that people who are on drugs are more likely to commit crimes than people who are not because of the chemical nature of the substances that are in those drugs. In other words, according to this view, the drugs themselves force drug users into crime. For purposes of challenging this argument, we will leave aside the issue of whether a person who uses drugs engages in crime to get the money needed to buy them. But a close look at the effects of drugs indicates that drug use need not cause criminal behavior.

There is no evidence that heroin and marijuana cause people to commit crime, however bad those substances are for one's health. It is true that cocaine is associated with crimes of violence because cocaine can result in depression, anxiety, and emotional instability. But it is unclear whether cocaine itself rather than withdrawal from cocaine produces these effects. If it is the latter, then decriminalization would allow a person addicted to cocaine to obtain the drug, which in turn would reduce those feelings that contribute to violent behavior.

Denial of drugs far less dangerous than cocaine can also produce criminal behavior so long as people crave that drug. The state of Vermont prohibited smoking in its prisons in the summer of 1992. An illegal trade in cigarettes soon resulted in the prison causing the price of cigarettes to increase by 2,000 percent. Prisoners threatened to engage in violence to get cigarettes. In November 1992, Vermont abandoned its ban on tobacco use in prison.

Seventh, with decriminalization, many crimes that are now committed would either not occur or else would be less likely to occur. In this regard, most of the homicides associated with drugs involve conflicts over drug deals and locations to sell drugs—not as a result of drug use itself. Victims of these conflicts are often members of inner-city minorities, some of whom are innocent bystanders.

Eighth, the criminalization of drugs undermines respect for law itself. For example, when a crack house operates in a neighborhood, sometimes people living nearby engage in vigilantism—the process of using illegal means for a public purpose—and burn down the house. No law-enforcement officials are involved in this act, so it is an act of lawlessness. And the widespread disrespect for drug laws results in disrespect for other laws as well. So many people violate the drug laws that citizens might easily believe that breaking the law is OK. In this way, even good citizens may show disrespect for law and in so doing undermine a key foundation of an ordered and just society.

Ninth, it is true that drug addicts often become involved in crimes. But to say that they engage in crime because they need money to feed their habit ignores factors that have nothing to do with drugs. In many cases, people on drugs were criminals before they even became addicts. They robbed people and stole property because they were criminals, not because they were drug addicts. If they did not rob and steal to buy narcotics, they would rob and steal to buy alcohol, food, and clothes.

Tenth, the criminal justice system can turn small-time users of drugs into big-time criminals. According to writer William Weir, three-quarters of all the people arrested for drug crimes in the United States are charged with simple possession. For some of these people who serve time in jail, the only crime they have ever committed was using drugs for themselves. But when they are in jail, they meet other inmates who have engaged in all kinds of crime, including contract murder and theft. Such associations can easily produce harmful consequences. According to Weir: "[T]here's a good chance that a person can go into jail as a simple drug user and come out prepared to support his habit in a comprehensive variety of illegal and violent ways."

Consequences to society. In addition to causing an increase in crime, the drug laws are responsible for other horrible social consequences. First, one of the worst consequences is that doctors are not prescribing strong enough painkillers and other medications for people who are suffering and need them. The most effective analgesic drugs (drugs used to relieve pain) are opiates (morphine, heroin, Dilaudid, and codeine) and methadone. But doctors and nurses know that DEA officials will harass them for prescribing opiates even for sound medical reasons, forcing unnecessary suffering on the part of sick or dying patients.

The drug laws not only force doctors to avoid giving the care that some of their patients need, but they turn innocent people who are suffering from illness into criminals. Marijuana is a case in point. Because marijuana is illegal, people who need it for medical reasons are subject to arrest. Marijuana relieves the symptoms of glaucoma, which can cause blindness. It has other medical uses, such as easing the pain in treatments for cancer and multiple sclerosis (a disease of the central nervous system). It helps AIDS patients, too. Every year, some users of marijuana for medical purposes are jailed. Even when Californians voted in favor of a statewide legalization of marijuana for medical needs in 1996, federal officials involved in enforcing drug laws denounced the proposition and promised to fight it.

This man is one of the few people in the country allowed to use marijuana for medical reasons. He is holding the can of marijuana that he receives every month from the U.S. government.

Second, drug laws are responsible for creating criminal behavior in neighborhoods, making areas unsafe, and lowering property values. People in inner cities cannot go out on the streets at night for fear that they will be cut down in the crossfire of one gang's drug war against another gang over which one can sell drugs in a particular location. It is not drugs themselves that do this, but rather drug laws as a result of their encouragement of criminal behavior in the dealing of drugs through the promise of earning quick money.

Third, drug laws are an important factor in destroying family life. Parents who are caught using or dealing in drugs are put in prison where they cannot do the nurturing that children in the inner cities and elsewhere so desperately need. Kids grow up in single-parent households or are shipped from one household to another, often to become part of a new generation involved in the drug trade and engaged in drug abuse. And drug laws destroy families in another way: by turning individuals against their own families. In 1986, for example, Deanna Young, a junior high school student in California, walked into a police station in California and turned in a bag containing an ounce of cocaine and small amounts of marijuana and pills. She had done so after attending an antidrug lecture. The police arrested and jailed her father and mother.

Fourth, drug laws damage people's health. People who need drugs cannot be sure that the drugs they are using are safe. Government could serve a great social good if it produced or licensed drugs that are now illegal. Because the manufacture of drugs is illegal, there are no quality controls for these substances. When a person buys a legal product in a supermarket, he or she can expect that the ingredients listed on the container accurately describe its contents and that the product itself is safe. If it is dangerous, the label will mention that fact. Failure to correctly list the ingredients or provide appropriate warnings about safety would likely be discovered by regulatory government agencies, resulting in the forced removal of the product and possibly a shutdown of the plant that made it. But since illegal drugs are not subject to government inspection, the quality of the product is not regulated. Poisonous substances can easily get into the product, resulting in the death or injury of the people who are unlucky enough to have consumed it.

The experience of alcohol prohibition in the United States shows much about the quality of products that have become criminalized. During Prohibition, thousands of Americans died or were blinded by contaminated alcohol they consumed. When the Soviet Union attempted to make it very difficult for citizens to get alcohol between 1985 and 1988, it showed similar results. In 1988, the last year of this partial prohibition, 40,000 Russians were poisoned, and 11,000 died.

Fifth, laws on decriminalization can be written in a manner that will prevent needless lawsuits over responsibility for any injury that a person on drugs may cause. The example of alcohol and the law is instructive. Alcohol is legal, but the law about the damage that an individual under the influence of alcohol causes is quite clear.

Sixth, decriminalization of drugs would not harm people in the inner cities more than others. Facts show, for example, that more white Americans use crack than do African Americans. (See Chapter 6.) But the law punishes black crack users in much larger proportion than it does white crack users.

Alternatives. Drug abuse is a great problem, but there are better ways to deal with it than through making it a crime. First, the best way to consider drug abuse is that it is a medical problem, not a criminal one. As such, the cure for drug abuse should be treatment and not punishment. Drug abuse itself is enough of a punishment. In this regard, conservative columnist William F. Buckley, Jr. calculates that treatment is seven times more cost-effective (economical) in reducing drug abuse than putting drug users into prison.

Second, at the minimum, the government could decriminalize marijuana. Marijuana is a "soft" drug compared to the hard drugs of heroin and cocaine. Unlike heroin and cocaine, marijuana does not kill. It is virtually impossible to overdose on marijuana. It is not as addictive as these other two drugs, and most people who smoke marijuana do not go on to hard drugs. It is true that marijuana affects the central nervous system and damages the lungs. But alcohol affects the central nervous system, too. We do not criminalize alcohol because it affects the central nervous system. And cigarettes contain tar, which when inhaled affects the lungs, but we do not make smoking cigarettes a crime either.

The Marijuana Commission formed during the administration of President Nixon found that "there is little proven danger of physical or psychological harm from the experimental or intermittent use" of marijuana. It recommended decriminalization of possession of marijuana for personal use on both the state and federal levels. The National Academy of Sciences issued a report in 1982 that found "no convincing evidence" that marijuana damages the brain or nervous system, or decreases fertility. Removing marijuana from the substance-abuse list would allow police to concentrate on other much-needed crime fighting. At present the police effort against marijuana use takes a good deal of their time. Marijuana offenses alone account for 450,000 arrests a year.

Opponents of marijuana have invented a "gateway theory" to scare people against decriminalization of this substance. The gateway theory asserts that when individuals use a weak drug, such as marijuana, they go on to use more powerful drugs like cocaine and heroin. Therefore, opponents of decriminalizing marijuana say, by decriminalizing marijuana use, the government is preparing the way to hard-drug addiction.

But studies of addiction show that the percentage of people who move from marijuana to cocaine and heroin is small, maybe in the single digits. Moreover, many of the people who are users of cocaine and heroin began their use of drugs with alcohol and tobacco. But opponents of decriminalizing marijuana do not ask for the banning of those drugs. They know the historical experience of banning alcohol. And they understand that most people who use alcohol and tobacco do not become addicted to hard drugs.

If the gateway theory were true, then we would expect to find that hard-drug use increased in step with marijuana use. But the evidence does not support this view. Marijuana use in the United States has risen enormously in the past few decades so that today there are an estimated 70 million pot smokers. But the number of heroin users today is about 500,000, about the same as it was in 1970.

Third, we need to have better educational programs showing the dangers of drugs. When people understand the dangers of something, they are likely to pay attention, but the message must be loud and clear. Education is responsible for the decline in the use of alcohol and tobacco. Organizations, such as Mothers Against Drunk Driving (MADD), have warned about the dangers of driving under the influence of alcohol. Medical authorities point to the threat excessive alcohol drinking poses to good health. For decades, health professionals have warned that tobacco may contribute to heart disease and cancer. Americans have responded by reducing the amount of tobacco that they consume. They have reduced alcohol consumption, too. The National Institute on Drug Abuse and Alcoholism reported, for example, that in 1994 American per capita (person) consumption of alcohol

Organizations such as MADD educate people about the dangers of driving drunk.

sank to its lowest level in 32 years. People are not stupid and have begun using these substances more wisely than they did before.

Thanks to public-interest advertising and educational campaigns, even drug addicts who use needles to inject drugs into their veins understand that the risk of getting AIDS from using unclean needles is high. In some U.S. cities, many of these addicted people have participated in needle-exchange programs in which they received clean needles in exchange for used, dirty ones. The number of AIDS cases has shown a decline in cities where this sensible policy has been adopted.

It is true that with decriminalization some people will become drug addicts. Many people now become alcoholics and tobacco addicts. But we cannot expect any public policy to help everyone. We have to do what is reasonable and has the best public consequences. Decriminalization of drugs would provide the best public consequences.

No. Drugs do so much damage that it is surprising that there are people in the United States who want to repeal the existing system of drug laws and usher in an experiment in decriminalization. Decriminalization would be disastrous. The arguments used to defend decriminalization are simply wrong.

Demand. If the United States engages in decriminalization, there will be an increase in drug use so enormous that we will have a drug epidemic incapable of being controlled. The damage in terms of death, poor health, and emotional disturbance will be shocking. In a decriminalized world, adults will be able to buy drugs at a government store or institution, and possibly, depending on the specific form of decriminalization, at a private business (maybe even a coffeehouse). A person will, then, have no fear that the taking of drugs will result in the kind of punishment that the criminal justice system now requires. Should anybody seriously believe that such easy availability will lead to a reduction in drug use? Why should it?

We have enough evidence to realize that increased drug availability leads to increased drug demand. During the Vietnam War, dealers made heroin available at a low price to American military personnel stationed in

Southeast Asia. The result was a drug epidemic that ruined many American lives. But one does not have to turn to the example of war to find evidence of what availability of drugs can do to people. One of the groups that has a high amount of drug use is health-care professionals—specifically doctors, nurses, and dentists. They have access to drugs as a result of their need to use them in medical practice for the medical needs of patients. But the fact that health-care professionals have easy access to legal drugs has resulted in their own abuse of drugs to a greater extent than professionals in other sectors of society. Medical people well understand that they can lose their license and be subject to severe criminal penalties if they are caught using drugs illegally, but some of them are willing to take the risk.

The experience of drug availability in countries other than the United States is scary. Since Peru became a major producer of cocaine and Colombia grew and processed cocaine in large amounts, both countries developed large addict populations. According to writer Jill Jonnes, the same is true of Pakistan: "Pakistan had virtually no heroin problem before the 1980s when the Afghan guerrillas and corrupt local officials flooded the nation with heroin. But in only three years, Pakistan had 1.3 million heroin addicts. In comparison the United States has 100,000 heroin addicts and three times the population of Pakistan." And *New York Times* columnist A. M. Rosenthal notes: "Italy, which decriminalized possession of heroin in 1975, now leads Western Europe in per capita heroin addiction, with 350,000 addicts."

Another reason to think that demand will increase with softer drug laws is that with decriminalization, many people will believe that taking drugs is OK. There will be no stigma (mark of disgrace) attached to drug use because the law says that taking drugs is not bad. What good would antidrug educational programs and commercials do if people understood that the government was not really serious about strengthening law enforcement in drug use?

Drug laws work to reduce demand. Surveys show that drug use is down considerably since the 1960s, and this reduction owes much to drug laws. The military is a good example because it has strict rules on drugs. Today, only about 3 percent of soldiers, sailors, and officers test positive for drugs. But a few decades ago—before the military got tough on the issue—about half of the members of the armed services tested positive for marijuana, while a quarter tested positive for other illegal drugs.

In a decriminalized drug world, addicts could feed their habit and increase their addiction just by going down the street and buying drugs openly. It is likely that they will do just that even more than they currently do in the illegal drug market. In this respect, demand will be increased further by the very nature of the drugs themselves. People who take certain drugs, such as cocaine, are likely to develop a dependency on them so that their tolerance declines. The more drugs they take, the more they need. Because decriminalization would make the drugs available with ease, it is likely that more casual drug users will become unable to control their habit and will increase their demand for drugs.

Finally, one should not underestimate the effect of price on demand. If drugs are decriminalized, the price of these substances would decline, making them affordable to more people. People who would not now have the money to try them even on an experimental basis because of cost would then be tempted to do so. We have a recent example from crack, which was developed as a way to increase sales by reaching people of limited income. The business strategy worked. Many people could afford a $3 to $5 vial of crack because it was cheap. The result was an epidemic of crack use in the inner cities.

Crime. Decriminalization would lead to an increase in crime. First, drug laws do not turn sane people into junkies (addicts), but drugs do. Many—if not most—addicts were involved in crime even before they became addicts, and drugs only made their criminal activity brutal and dangerous to others. If drugs become more easily available, these criminals will act ever so much more recklessly.

Second, the experience of countries outside the United States should give some guidance in adopting public policy. In the mid-1980s, for example, Zurich, Switzerland, opened "Needle Park," to which drug users could come. The police view was that it was better to have drug users in one place. But before long, 20,000 drug users were there—many from countries outside of Switzerland. Crime increased in the community near the park, and the Zurich City Council closed the park.

Third, most supporters of decriminalization draw the line where young people are affected. If they achieved their goal, law-enforcement officials would still punish anyone selling drugs to young people. But with decriminalization, drug criminals would be able to concentrate their efforts on America's vulnerable youth simply because young people would become their last big illegal market. And decriminalization would hurt kids in another way: With unlimited amounts of drugs available to adults, no doubt more adults would become addicted. Some of the adult addicts would probably engage in harmful activity against young people because of the violent behavior that some drugs cause. In this regard, former drug czar William J. Bennett points out: "In Philadelphia in 1987 more than half the child-abuse fatalities involved at least one parent who was a heavy drug user. Seventy-three percent of the child-abuse cases in New York City in 1987 involved parental drug use."

Fourth, crime would probably increase with decriminalization. With decriminalization, the cost of drugs would be low. Addicts would spend more time using drugs than working because the drugs would be inexpensive and available. The result would be that addicts would engage in crime simply to make a living. Dr. Herbert D. Kleber of the Center on Addiction and Substance Abuse at Columbia University says in this regard that the total number of addicts may increase and so, too, would the amount of crime. He observes: "Fewer crimes would be committed by each addict, but there would be substantially more crime overall."

Fifth, the idea that with decriminalization of drugs, the police will be able to use their limited resources to fight other forms of violent and criminal behavior is an illusion. As indicated above, with decriminalization, crime will increase rather than decrease. Decriminalization of drugs would result in the police becoming less capable of dealing with other forms of criminal

In the mid-1980s, Zurich, Switzerland, opened "Needle Park," to which drug users could come.

behavior because they will be overwhelmed with dealing with crimes committed by people on drugs.

Sixth, decriminalization will not result in the end of crime by law-enforcement officials. Most law-enforcement officials in the United States are honest and do the tough jobs of fighting crime that put their lives at risk. But there will always be people who are willing to betray the public trust for their private greed. Long before drugs were made illegal in the United States, some law-enforcement officials were taking bribes and aiding criminals in violation of the law. People will be offering bribes to law-enforcement officials whether they want to have a traffic ticket fixed or a serious crime ignored.

Seventh, advocates of decriminalization often make no distinction in the drugs that they would decriminalize. But some drugs cause people to act violently. Crack is a case in point. To the extent that people could easily obtain such drugs at will, then an increased amount of violent behavior would probably result.

Eighth, it is true that people who disobey the drug laws show a disrespect for law in general. But that is no more an argument for legalizing drug laws than it is for legalizing bank robbery, rape, and murder because people who commit those deeds show a disrespect for law, too.

Ninth, it is true that small-time criminals placed in prisons could learn how to become hardened criminals. But that is no more true for those who break drug laws than it is for those who break other laws. Sentencing guidelines determine the penalty for each kind of offense. Usually, small-time drug users who are caught for the first time in their drug violation do not go to jail anyway. If they get a sentence to serve time, they probably have not learned their lesson. In addition, the solution to the problem of the use of jails and prisons as crime schools is to create better institutions for holding prisoners and more alert corrections officers but not to get rid of the criminal laws.

Consequences to society. Decriminalization of drugs will be harmful to society in many ways other than increasing crime. First, decriminalization will result in a decline in health for many people, as the evidence about health during Prohibition shows. Alcohol is responsible for many cases of cirrhosis—a disease of the liver that results in liver failure and death. During Prohibition, the number of deaths from this disease dropped. For example, Mark H. Moore, a professor of criminal justice at Harvard's Kennedy School of Government, points to evidence that cirrhosis death rates for men dropped from 29.5 per 100,000 in 1911 to 10.7 in 1929. Additionally, he claims, "Admissions to state mental hospitals for alcoholic psychosis declined from 10.1 per 100,000 in 1919 to 4.7 in 1928."

Second, drugs are not a victimless crime. They produce victims other than the people who take them. Pregnant drug addicts bring babies into the world who are often underweight, mentally damaged, and have the virus that causes AIDS. Some of these babies require medical care and special educational programs for the rest of their lives—usually at great public expense. Drugs are often responsible for broken homes and spouse and child abuse. Workers who are on drugs are more likely to cause accidents than workers who are not, and in so doing are a threat to the safety of other people.

Third, there will be more homeless people as greater and greater numbers of people will suffer from the effects of drugs and become more incapable of working and paying the rent or mortgage. We have only to walk along the streets of big cities to see the many people who camp out in alleyways and parks because drugs have made them incapable of functioning effectively.

Fourth, decriminalization would result in many legal problems. If someone—whether government official or private citizen—supplies cocaine to another person, who as a result of the drugs acts violently, who would be legally responsible for that crime? The answer to that question would turn the legal system into a nightmare as the number of lawsuits would skyrocket.

Fifth, the attempt to equate alcohol with hard drugs is wrong. Drugs have a more horrible impact than alcohol on society. People who do hard drugs are likely to want to get high. As such, they are likely to act in an antisocial manner. But most people who take alcohol do not seek to get high. They take a drink at the end of the day to ease the pressures of the moment. One or two drinks is all they consume. They are not likely to act in an antisocial manner.

It is true that people can become addicted to alcohol or hard drugs. But a person becomes an alcoholic usually in a few years. In comparison, a person becomes a drug addict in a few weeks or months. In addition, most alcoholics can work and live without difficulty when they are not consuming alcohol. But most addicts are unable to function in a normal manner any time that they are awake.

Sixth, inner-city African Americans would be most hurt if recent patterns of drug addiction are any indication of future behavior. Crack, which is both cheap and available, took a heavy toll in the inner cities. And opening up the opportunity to get more drugs easily and at a low price would be devastating to African Americans trapped in poor and hopeless situations.

Seventh, the charge that doctors are ignoring their medical responsibilities by not prescribing a drug, such as marijuana, to solve medical problems is not true. For legal drugs are available that can achieve the same results as marijuana. For example, Marinol, which is made from cannabis, is a legal drug and contains the essential ingredient of THC. Marinol can be used to treat appetite and weight loss experienced by people with AIDS. It can also be used to treat cancer patients. Many people who launch campaigns to legalize drugs for medical use are not really interested in their medical use but want to make them so easily available that anybody can get them merely by claiming to have some medical problem.

Alternatives. The proposed alternatives to making drugs a crime will not work. First, the case for treatment as an alternative to criminal justice ignores the ways in which individuals obtain treatment. There is no conflict between treatment and law enforcement. Taking people out of the criminal justice system might remove them from treatment. According to ONDCP, prison-based drug treatment has been shown to be an effective means of controlling both drug use and recidivism (returning to criminal behavior). Offenders serving long-term jail and prison sentences can often get attention for their addiction in therapeutic communities. There are other means of care that are also part of criminal justice treatment. For nonviolent offenders without a criminal record, drug courts have shown great potential for dealing with drug abuse. In these programs, a drug user can stay free provided he or she gets treatment and stays clear of drugs. These programs are under court supervision. Drug court programs in Fort Lauderdale, Florida; Miami, Florida; Oakland, California; Portland, Oregon; New York City; and the District of Columbia have shown progress in helping people keep away from drugs.

Second, advocates of decriminalization ask at a minimum that marijuana be decriminalized. But their claim that marijuana is not a harmful drug is wrong. Marijuana is a dangerous drug. It is a carcinogen (a cancer-causing substance) that contains twice the amount of tar than is found in tobacco. Cannabis is toxic (poisonous). It affects the central nervous system, the lungs, and the immunity and reproductive functions in a harmful way. It is rare that a person who is hooked on hard drugs has never used cannabis before. It is wrong to consider marijuana a "soft" drug compared to the "hard" drugs of heroin and cocaine.

Third, education is not a substitute for law enforcement. Nobody is arguing that the nation should end drug-education programs. They do influence behavior. But so, too, do antidrug laws. With decriminalization, people would tend to ignore the educational message since the message on the television programs they receive that say "Don't do drugs" would be different from the unspoken but powerful message that they get from law-enforcement officials that says: "It is OK to do drugs."

The advocates of decriminalization, although often well-intentioned, would produce a policy that will wreck lives. We have made a lot of progress under the current system of drug laws and penalties. We would only destroy that progress if we try the decriminalization experiment.

Chapter 5
DRUG LAWS AND CIVIL LIBERTIES

Debate: Are Drug Laws a Threat to Civil Liberties?

Because the men who established the American system of government in the late 18th century feared that a powerful government could threaten individual liberties, they created a system of limited government. Under this system, government would have power to make and carry out laws, but it could not do just anything it wanted. One way that people would have protection against government was through a system of individual rights, or civil liberties, that were written into the Constitution and the Bill of Rights (the first ten amendments of the Constitution). Some state constitutions had their own bills of rights, too, which assured civil liberties for the people who lived in those states. As written, the rights in the Constitution and Bill of Rights were protections against the federal government, not the states. Since 1925, however, the Supreme Court extended most of the rights so as to assure protection against the state governments, as well.

Among the rights assured by the federal government are protections against government interference in stopping people from speaking about political and other subjects, practicing their religious faith, or reporting the news. Rights of individuals accused of a crime are also assured. These include protection against unreasonable searches and seizures, the right to have an attorney in one's defense, no double jeopardy (putting someone on trial for an offense for which that person has already been put on trial), and due process (protection against the government from acting to deny an individual life, liberty, or property beyond what the law allows).

But rights are not absolutes. Under certain conditions, government may take action to limit rights when some important public purpose is regarded as more worthy than the rights themselves. Freedom of religion, for example, does not permit an individual to sacrifice the life of another individual even if such a practice is in accord with one's religious beliefs. And government may place some restrictions on freedom of the press during wartime in the interest of national security.

The Supreme Court is the institution that interprets the Constitution, and among its responsibilities is to make the determination as to whether the government has acted in a manner to threaten or damage civil liberties. At times it decides for government, and at other times for the citizen who is challenging the government. Sometimes, in considering a constitutional matter, the Court establishes a principle that has lasting consequences for civil liberties. The Supreme Court has, for example, found that a right of privacy exists, although it is not specifically mentioned in the Constitution or Bill of Rights. Such a right means that one has the power to determine one's personal affairs free from governmental interference and may control the distribution of information about oneself.

As federal, state, and local governments have passed laws to control the trafficking and use of drugs, they have engaged in practices involving the conflict between government conduct and individual liberty. The courts have had to decide whether these drug laws go beyond what the Constitution allows. In this chapter we consider only a few of the issues raised in cases dealing with drugs: specifically, those involving forfeiture, searches and seizures, and privacy rights for individuals taking drug tests.

DEBATED:

ARE DRUG LAWS A THREAT TO CIVIL LIBERTIES?

Yes. At its core, the war on drugs is an assault on individual liberties. Government has passed laws that interfere with rights long accepted in American society, as may be seen in the way it has acted in matters involving forfeiture, searches and seizures, and drug tests.

Forfeiture. Under the American system of law, government may under certain conditions forfeit property from an individual. Although forfeiture laws have been on the books in the United States for centuries, the war on drugs has extended government's power to the point at which government has violated civil liberties.

There are two kinds of forfeiture laws: civil forfeiture and criminal forfeiture. As its name implies, civil forfeiture is tried under principles of civil law that determine property rights. Criminal forfeiture is tried under principles of criminal law that determine liberty rights. Civil forfeiture is the older form of forfeiture; criminal forfeiture dates back only to 1970. In civil law cases, before people are deprived of their property, they are entitled to a civil trial. The standard of proof in such a trial is known as "preponderance of the evidence," which means the stronger and more convincing evidence of contending parties to a dispute. In civil forfeiture trials, the litigants (the persons engaged in a lawsuit) may have counsel (an attorney) but generally must hire their own attorneys at their own expense.

In criminal forfeiture cases, an individual is entitled to a criminal trial in which the standard for winning a case is "beyond a reasonable doubt." This is a tougher standard than "preponderance of the evidence." In criminal cases, individuals have a right to an attorney. If defendants do not have sufficient money to pay for an attorney, then the government provides one for them at public expense.

A number of federal laws in recent decades have dealt with forfeiture. In 1970, Congress passed the Racketeer Influenced and Corrupt Organization Act (RICO). A part of that law, which targeted organized crime, allowed prosecutors to confiscate much more broadly than it had before. With criminal forfeiture, RICO permitted prosecutors to take away not only the illegal product but products associated with it no matter who owned them. In 1978, Congress authorized the seizure and forfeiture of anything of value used or intended to be used in exchange for illegal drugs, all money used or intended to be used to facilitate (make easier) any illegal drug transaction, and all "proceeds traceable" to an illegal drug exchange. And the Comprehensive Crime Control Act of 1984 added to the list of items to be forfeited "all real property... which is used or intended to be used... to commit or facilitate the commission" of any felony (major crime) under the Controlled Substances Act. State governments adopted their own forfeiture laws, too. From 1985 to 1991, the number of federal seizures of property under forfeiture laws increased by 1,500 percent.

The government has preferred to rely on civil forfeiture in its war on drugs. Under civil forfeiture laws, the property—rather than the individual—is

Cars are often seized by police as forfeiture in drug cases.

accused of a crime. When individuals are accused of a crime, they have legal protections. But as a thing rather than a person, the property has no civil liberties protection, and the government may take possession of the property even if a person who owns the property is not accused of a crime. The government only needs to present evidence of "probable cause" to seize the property. The "probable cause" may be based on rumor, gossip, or informants. The identity of the informants is often kept confidential so that the person whose property is seized does not face an accuser. The person who owns the property then must sue to get it back by showing that it was seized unjustly. The owner must prove that he or she lacked both control of the property when it was unlawfully used and knowledge of its unlawful use.

The forfeiture laws are violations of civil liberties for many Americans and challenge the protection of property that is supposed to be assured by the Fifth and Fourteenth amendments to the Constitution. The Fifth Amendment states that private property shall not "be taken for public use without just compensation." The Fourteenth Amendment adds: "nor shall any State deprive any person of life, liberty, or property, without due process of law." In addition, the Sixth Amendment to the Constitution states that an accused shall enjoy the right "to be confronted with the witnesses against him." But these are rights in criminal matters. Because civil forfeiture is a matter of civil law, the individual whose property has been seized does not have these rights. What is particularly harmful to civil liberties is that under the drug forfeiture laws, the owner must prove that he or she is innocent, where in criminal proceedings the burden of proof is on the government.

Sometimes, individuals may lose the use of property even when they have done nothing wrong. A law-abiding and non-drug using individual who owns a car and lends it to his or her son may discover that the police have seized the car when they discovered the driver with drugs in the vehicle. Moreover, mere suspicion that an individual is involved in drugs can result in punishment. Police took $9,000 in cash that a woman was carrying in her car because they suspected that the $9,000 was going to be used for drugs. In fact, the money had nothing to do with drugs. But the woman had to prove her innocence. She had no criminal record, and no drugs were in her car. She received only part of the money back as a result of her hiring an attorney because she had to pay her expenses in pursuing the matter.

Under federal rules, once the property is seized, the government takes control of it until the case is completed. A person has ten days to make a claim to get the property or money back. That means that the individual must hire an attorney to follow the appropriate legal procedures. The property owner must pay 10 percent of the value of the property as a bond (security) within 30 days or less to have any court remedies. Some people lose their property because they cannot afford to hire attorneys. In civil forfeiture cases, poor people are penalized because they are not entitled to a government-appointed attorney.

Under the drug laws, government can through the forfeiture proceedings seize a person's home, bank account, records, and property without a trial. Congressman Henry Hyde, chairman of the House Judiciary Committee, points out in his book on forfeiture that 80 percent of the people whose property is seized by the federal government under drug laws are never formally charged with any crime. Many of those people simply could not afford to hire an attorney. At the minimum, government should furnish them with an attorney, as it does in criminal matters.

Even when people succeed in getting their forfeited property back, they may suffer great losses. Property is sometimes held for months and as a result becomes damaged. In the care of law-enforcement officials, homes seized by government in forfeiture proceedings have been vandalized, and boats have fallen into disrepair. Owners have to spend thousands of dollars to pay for the repairs. And the owners do not have the legal authority to require government to pay for any damage that was caused while the property was under its control. In effect, government destroyed or damaged their property without due process of law, a clear violation of a civil liberty. At the minimum, an individual so injured should have the right to sue the government for negligence—the failure to take reasonable care.

People who suffer from forfeiture wonder about the intentions of law-enforcement officials. There is much that is self-serving in the forfeiture laws. The federal law permits law-enforcement agencies to keep the proceeds and property they seize and forfeit. They must use these funds and property for law-enforcement purposes. But unlike the funds provided by government for law enforcement, elected public officials do not oversee how these funds are used. According to news reports, some of these funds are used for questionable purposes. Because they benefit directly from forfeiture, the police have an incentive to go after property, and some local law-enforcement authorities have been particularly aggressive in using forfeiture to build up law-enforcement budgets.

Finally, the whole notion that civil forfeiture attacks the illegal drug industry is phony. Even if the entire billion dollars in forfeitures that is seized every year came from persons in the drug business (a false assumption because it comes from many sources), this figure represents less than 2 percent of America's illegal drug market. Drug traffickers can afford to pay such a small price.

Searches and seizures. The Fourth Amendment to the Constitution provides that "the right of the people to be secure in their persons, houses, papers, and effects, against unreasonable searches and seizures, shall not be violated...." But in the past few decades, federal and state governments have become aggressive about the war on drugs at the expense of the individual's right to be protected against unreasonable searches and seizures.

The Fourth Amendment provides that a search warrant is required in order to conduct a search under certain conditions. A search warrant is a written order by a court that directs a law-enforcement official to search for a specific item in a particular place and to seize it if it is there. The item may be stolen goods, contraband (illegal imports), or physical evidence of the commission of a crime. A warrant is not needed if it can be shown that time or circumstances did not reasonably permit securing it. As a result of the war on drugs, warrants are often obtained on the basis of anonymous tips and tips from informants who are known to be corrupt. And the courts have even upheld the issuance of a defective search warrant if the police acted in "good faith."

Thanks also to the drug crusade, the police now conduct searches without warrants. Without a warrant, police may now search luggage, trash cans, car interiors, bus passengers, fenced private property, and barns. Police helicopters fly over areas they suspect are being used to grow illicit crops or manufacture illegal drugs. On the basis of what they see from the air, the police then get a warrant. Police are allowed to search people's garbage in an effort to locate evidence of drugs. Drug testing is a search, too, and the courts have upheld the legality of requiring such tests for government and some private employees. (See p. 75.)

Young people in particular are vulnerable to searches by the police in violation of their privacy. In schools, they are subject to unannounced searches of their lockers and personal effects—all without a warrant. In some cases, students have even been strip-searched.

The police stop cars at roadblocks and search them without a warrant. They stop people who are passengers at airports or who are passengers in a car on interstate highways merely because they fit a profile (description) of the features and behavior of presumed typical drug couriers (messengers). Profiles are so vague as to give authorities great discretion in searching. In effect, they can search anyone they want to search. For example, at airports, profiles of suspicious people have included: flying one-way or round trip, flying nonstop or stopping, and flying alone or with someone. Often, the profile includes a disproportionate percentage of racial minorities, particularly Hispanics and African Americans. Once stopped,

Police use dogs that sniff school lockers for drugs.

the police can have dogs sniff the baggage and pockets of a suspect to determine whether that individual is carrying drugs. If the police suspect that a traveler from a foreign country entering the United States has swallowed a balloon containing drugs, they may order the person to remain with them until that individual defecates over a wastebasket under the observation of law-enforcement officials.

Drug testing. The American system of law and justice rests on basic principles of rights that have served the nation well. Among these principles are: Defendants are presumed innocent until proven guilty, and individuals have a right of privacy. In applying the principle of a presumption of innocence, the government must prove that a suspected criminal has broken the law. The individual does not have to prove his or her innocence. A defendant cannot be forced to testify if he or she does not wish to do so. In the matter of privacy, the Supreme Court has interpreted the Constitution to indicate that this right exists.

Drug tests threaten these fundamental rights. A close look at the procedure of drug tests shows their danger to rights. People who are required to take tests may actually be giving evidence that can be used against them. If, for example, they have smoked marijuana on Saturday night for recreational purposes, traces of marijuana will remain in their bodies for weeks. When those individuals show up for work on Monday, they are ready and able to do their jobs without any trace of impairment in the performance of their jobs. But the drug tests will reveal that the individuals are guilty of taking drugs. In short, the individuals had to supply the evidence that is used against them—a real slap in the face of the American system of law and justice. Worse yet, tests using people's hair will disclose if they took drugs several months earlier, and the workers who did take drugs could be dismissed although they stopped taking drugs three months before the test.

With the possibility of drug tests always at hand, individuals must always be on their guard lest they display behavior patterns that a supervisor might mistakenly consider to be suspicious. Even organizations that do not routinely use random testing rely on tests when there is "probable cause" of impairment. Such cause may be frequent lateness, mood changes, and absenteeism. It is true that people hooked on drugs may show these qualities. But it is also true that sometimes people may have other problems that produce similar effects. For example, a person who is sleeping on the job may have been up all night caring for a sick family member. Or the mood changes and absenteeism may result from personal problems at home. Yet that person may be forced to prove his or her innocence by a job-required drug test.

One of the serious violations of rights is that some people who test positive for drugs are never even told that the reason that they do not get a job is because they test positive. This is particularly true for new applicants for jobs, some of whom only get one test. Only a few states require that drug test results be sent directly to the applicant.

People who must take drug tests are forced to give up some basic rights of privacy, too. First, they must disclose the legal drugs that they are taking because such drugs may include substances that will show up in the tests as illegal. A person on methadone, a legal drug, will in effect inform an employer that he or she is a former heroin addict although that individual may be functioning quite well on the job precisely because of methadone treatment. Similarly, a person may be taking marijuana to help control glaucoma, or amphetamines to deal with depression, or opiate analgesics to relieve pain. The person who takes the test has no idea who will see the "private" medication report and, consequently, does not know whether knowledge of a health problem will have a bearing on continuing employment or promotion.

Second, someone must observe an individual giving a urine specimen lest the urine sample be tampered with or replaced with someone else's urine. It is humiliating enough to be required to urinate into a bottle to satisfy the requirements of a drug test. But there are official watchers to make certain that the sample is valid and has not been tampered with. The Office of Personnel Management, the office that supervises federal government employees, requires a monitor nearby, but this person does not actually observe people giving samples. The military, however, is more strict. According to a report in the *New York Times*, a representative of the armed forces said, "Oh, we don't fool around with any of that. We watch 'em."

Third, privacy is violated because the employee has no idea who will see the records. If a test reveals that a worker has used marijuana, for example, the test results may be sent from one employer to another employer considering hiring that person. In addition, the employee does not know whether the company is using the information from drug tests to detect employees with medical problems. Once such employees are identified, the company may encourage them to leave the organization.

The war on drugs has taken a heavy toll on the liberty of Americans. Congress has been willing to pass laws that violate civil liberties all for the cause of ending the illegal use of drugs—a purpose that has failed. And the courts have upheld police practices in searches and seizures. Unfortunately, the price to liberty is high. The injury done to civil liberties in the United States makes an observation of economist Friedrich von Hayek very perceptive. He wrote: "It is indeed probable that more harm and misery have been caused by men determined to use coercion to stamp out a moral evil than by men intent on doing evil."

No. Drugs are a threat to the life and health of all Americans. U.S. citizens recognize that threat and support officials for elected public office who are committed to waging war on drug trafficking and drug use. Those officials have written laws to deal with drug criminals. In matters of drug laws, the Supreme Court has determined that these laws are in most cases proper to deal with a major social problem and that they do not violate fundamental civil liberties. The application of laws involving forfeiture, searches and seizures, and drug tests are appropriate means to deal with a major issue of our times and do not violate civil liberties.

Forfeiture. Asset forfeiture has become the principal legal tool by which the government recovers money and property gained from the illegal trafficking and use of drugs. Asset forfeiture hits drug violators where it hurts the most: in their pockets. It attacks the economic incentive to engage in organized criminal activity. As a result of the forfeiture laws, government can take away planes and boats used to carry drugs as well as the homes used to make or store them. It can take away the money in the businesses and bank accounts that drug traffickers have made as a result of their illicit drug activities.

Critics of forfeiture laws often fail to point out that there is really nothing new about these laws. They were not invented to fight the war on drugs. Rather, forfeiture procedures in place today existed both before and after the Constitution was adopted. The first federal civil forfeiture law was enacted in 1789 by the very first Congress. And since the early 19th century, when John Marshall was the Chief Justice, the Supreme Court has upheld the constitutionality of forfeiture laws.

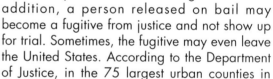

John Marshall (1755–1835)

Forfeiture is vital to law-enforcement authorities because it works in ways that other penalties, such as fines, do not. Fines are usually ineffective in getting at the economic assets of drug traffickers because fines can only be enforced after a person is convicted of a crime. By that time, the criminals have either spent all their assets or placed them beyond the reach of the government. In addition, a person released on bail may become a fugitive from justice and not show up for trial. Sometimes, the fugitive may even leave the United States. According to the Department of Justice, in the 75 largest urban counties in 1988, felony drug defendants were more likely than other defendants to remain fugitives for more than one year after failing to make an appearance. The collection rate of fines in federal court is only 6 percent. Because of civil forfeitures, however, the government has the ill-gotten criminal gains under its control so that when there is a conviction, the government can take over criminal assets and thus cause real damage to drug cartels.

Forfeiture laws differ between the federal and state governments and among state governments, so it is difficult to make generalizations that cover them all. But such laws do not violate civil liberties because they contain safeguards protecting innocent citizens. In federal forfeiture laws, for example, government must show probable cause in order to seize property.

That requirement forces the government to show that the property must be either the profits of, or the means to, facilitate or commit certain designated crimes. In addition, there are defenses in congressional laws that protect individuals. For example, even if the government shows that an automobile was used to transport drugs, the owner of the automobile can defeat the forfeiture by showing that he or she was not aware of the act nor consented to the illegal use of the car. And poor people are not victimized by the bond requirement. In both law and practice, people who can demonstrate that they are indigent (poor) can obtain a waiver of this requirement.

It is true that in some cases, law-enforcement officials do not take proper care of the property that they have seized. But these cases are few in number. Permitting individuals the right to sue the government for matters of negligence in dealing with the property seized in drug matters would destroy the criminal justice system. For it is reasonable to assume that the principle of allowing individuals the right to sue for negligence on a property seized for some drug-related matter would be extended to cover many other areas of government activity, as well. The number of lawsuits against government by individuals whose property is seized because they failed to pay their taxes or pay back their student loans would themselves pose an enormous burden on taxpayers.

The claim that individuals in civil forfeiture proceedings should be able to have attorneys provided to them has really nothing to do with civil liberties. Federal and state courts have rejected such a right in civil matters. In criminal matters, of course, people do have a right to counsel at government expense when they cannot afford to pay for one.

Critics point to the practice of reliance on informants as a violation of civil liberties. But such a charge ignores the necessity of using unnamed informants. The identity of informants is often kept confidential for a good reason. If the government revealed their identities, the informants would be in great danger from violent acts of revenge by drug traffickers. The knowledge that the identity of an informant would be known, moreover, would discourage other would-be informants from coming forward and offering tips to the police about drug violations.

The fact that proceeds from forfeitures go into law-enforcement treasuries should be praised rather than criticized. Between 1985 and 1993, the Justice Department transferred nearly $1.2 billion to more than 3,000 state and local law-enforcement agencies. Millions of dollars of these funds have been used to build prisons and jails and to pay for investigations and prosecution expenses in criminal cases. In addition, this money has been used for programs in drug abuse education and drug treatment, among other law-enforcement purposes. And the taxpayers have benefited because they did not have to pay these sums.

It is true that at times federal and state law-enforcement officials have made errors. But few mistakes are made and those that do occur get excessive media attention. Moreover, the Department of Justice took steps in 1993 to strengthen quality control in the forfeiture program and to minimize any bad effects of forfeiture on innocent persons. These steps include speeding up notice to owners of seized property and adopting a model code of professional conduct for asset forfeiture. In addition, forfeiture training programs for law-enforcement officials at the federal and state levels have improved the knowledge of those individuals about what they can and cannot do in forfeiture matters.

Searches and seizures. The Fourth Amendment forbids unreasonable searches and seizures. It does not define the meaning of "unreasonable," however. Nor could it do so given the varieties of situations in which crime occurs and the changing scope of criminal law. The Supreme Court has dealt with search and seizure on a case-by-case basis. But since the early 1970s, almost all the searches and seizures reaching the United States Supreme Court have been upheld, and with good reason, too.

Drug traffickers use a variety of techniques to smuggle and distribute their harmful and illegal products. The courts have correctly noted that in many situations, there is simply not enough time for police to obtain search warrants. Since the drug cartels use air, sea, and ground transportation to ship their goods, the courts have correctly regarded warrantless searches as constitutionally permitted. The courts understand the danger that drug supplies will get out of hand and destroy more lives. For example, estimates of the number of Americans who now grow marijuana in their homes range from 500,000 to 2,000,000. Such extensive activity justifies helicopter surveillance of property suspected to be involved in the growing of that substance. As mentioned above, the use of informants is invaluable to capture contraband and to prevent drug trafficking or to punish those engaged in the drug trade.

The use of profiles is a legitimate method for waging the war on drugs. To be sure, some police have used profiles in a racially discriminatory manner. But when such practices have been brought to the attention of the public, the police in many cases have been careful to create a new system of profiles that does not target racial minorities.

Young people are vulnerable to the allure of drugs. It is in their interest that law-enforcement officials conduct searches at schools. Drug traffickers in school need to be excluded from selling their products to other students, and searches of lockers and personal effects help achieve that goal. And if a student does use drugs, then early parental awareness may result in treatment before he or she becomes an addict.

The impression one gets from civil liberties advocates is that there are no limitations on the police in search and seizure matters. But that is not the case. Police cannot conduct searches at will unless they have a good legal reason to do so. Police can stop a vehicle. But they need to justify a pat down with a reasonable suspicion, which is more than a hunch. A person may be asked: "Can we search you?" And the answer can be "No." A person can consent to a limited search of an area. But if the police conduct a search in a manner that is not in accord with court interpretations, then a judge will rule that the evidence seized cannot be used in a trial.

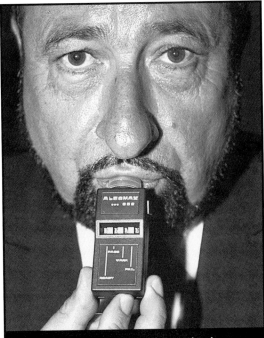

Federal courts have upheld the right to conduct drug tests, such as this alcohol breath analyzer.

Drug testing. Drug tests are not a violation of rights. The rights granted to Americans in the Bill of Rights are not absolute. The Fourth Amendment does not prevent all searches and seizures. It prevents only searches that are unreasonable. The courts have found, for example, that a person boarding an aircraft can be searched for explosives although that individual is not a person suspected of carrying explosives. Given the fact that terrorists and others have seized control of aircraft in flight, resulting in death and injury to passengers and crews, the courts regard such inspection as reasonable.

Federal courts have upheld the right to conduct drug tests. In 1989, the Supreme Court upheld drug tests to ensure public safety in two important cases: *Skinner v. Railway Labor Executives* and *National Treasury Employees Union v. Von Rabb*. In the Von Rabb case, the Supreme Court held that for jobs including public safety, drug-prevention missions, or people holding positions with access to truly sensitive material, a government agency may require drug tests although there is no suspicion that the person being tested has taken drugs. And the courts have expanded the use of drug tests. In 1995, for example, in *Veronia School District v. Acton*, the Supreme Court upheld the right of school districts to conduct random drug tests of student athletes.

Opponents of drug tests complain that the taking of drugs for recreational purposes ought to be of no concern to an employer if the worker is not impaired. A worker taking drugs on Saturday night can work without impairment on Monday. But some people who take certain drugs on a Saturday night and go to work on Monday suffer from the drugs' aftereffects when they are on the job on Monday. These people cause accidents in spite of the fact that a day and a half has gone by since they took the drug. A study by Jerome Yesavage of Stanford University, for example, showed that ten airplane pilots who had used marijuana on a simulator indicated impairment from the drug in their landing performance even 24 hours after use.

Employees have legitimate concerns about protecting their privacy, but the concerns of society regarding drug use are important, too. Americans must make a statement that any standard other than zero tolerance of drugs is not acceptable. The question is: Do we accept drug use or not? Drug testing sends a message at the workplace that drug use is unacceptable in any form. Unfortunately, in terms of privacy, urine tests are an excellent means for detecting drug use. But those tests are necessary to achieve a drug-free America.

It is not an easy matter for the Supreme Court to draw the line between the needs of law-enforcement officials to deal with a recognized threat to the safety and health of the American people and the liberty of individuals. But the Supreme Court has carefully considered the dangers in drawing that line.

Chapter 6
DRUGS AND RACIAL MINORITIES

Debate: Does Drug Policy Discriminate Against
Racial Minorities?

The criminal laws against drugs in the United States do not single
out any particular racial group as a target for punishment. In principle, any person who manufactures, distributes, or consumes illegal
drugs is subject to the criminal penalties set forth in those laws. In
practice, however, drug laws affect some racial groups more than
others. The criminal sentence for using one illegal substance consumed by an African-American or Latino group may be much
higher than the criminal sentence for using another illegal substance
consumed by another group. In this situation, the negatively affected
groups may feel that the laws have a racial aspect that does not
appear in the statutes. If the police and other law-enforcement officials carry out those laws against one racial group rather than
another, then the penalized racial group may feel that the very purpose of the drug law itself is to punish people because of their race.

Particularly since the 1980s, many people in the African-
American and Latino communities have become highly critical of
both the content of drug laws and the way that law-enforcement
authorities carry out the laws. In addition, they have raised questions
about whether the federal government is responsible for knowingly
allowing drugs into minority neighborhoods in the first place.

DEBATED:

DOES DRUG POLICY DISCRIMINATE AGAINST RACIAL MINORITIES?

Yes. The role of race in drug policy has been a feature of U.S. history for more than a century. California passed the first law against opium smuggling in response to claims made in the 1870s that the Chinese were drugging white women into sexual slavery. At the beginning of the 20th century, some southern sheriffs said that they were switching from .32- to .38-caliber pistols because the older guns were ineffective in stopping the "coke-crazed" black man. And marijuana was made illegal in 1937 in response to the claim that it was a "killer weed" that made smokers, particularly Mexicans, violent.

Today, racism—discrimination based on race—and drugs remain linked in spite of the changes in civil rights laws since the 1960s that are supposed to assure equal justice under law for all Americans. Racism in the drug laws can be seen from an analysis of the criminal justice system, penalties for crack, and the domestic and foreign policies of the United States that have an impact on drug availability and use.

Criminal justice system. By any standard, racial minorities, and particularly black people, suffer unfairly in the criminal justice system. Drug laws are a major factor in legal discrimination. Between 1983 and 1993, the number of incarcerated (imprisoned) drug offenders increased in the United States from 57,000 to 353,000. The black proportion of drug arrests rose from 24 percent in 1980 to 39 percent by 1993, according to Marc Mauer, assistant director of the Sentencing Project, a Washington, D.C.-based nonprofit organization that promotes sentencing reform and conducts research on criminal justice issues.

In a fair and just system, one would expect that there would be some relationship between seriousness of particular drug crimes on the one hand and the harshness of sentences of the people who commit those crimes on the other. But that is not the case for black Americans. Citing information covering 1992 and 1993 that appeared in government sources, the Sentencing Project calculates that African Americans represent 12 percent of the population, 13 percent of drug users, 35 percent of arrests for drug possession, 55 percent of convictions for drug possession, and 74 percent of prison sentences for drug possession. The Sentencing Project also notes that African Americans and Hispanics combined now make up nearly 90 percent of all offenders sentenced to state prisons for drug offenses. As Dr. Robert Newman of Beth Israel Hospital in New York City said: "If, instead of 95 percent of all inmates in New York being black and Hispanic, half were white, somebody long ago would have said: 'What are you doing? You can't lock up the youth of America.'"

The Sentencing Project issued a report in 1995 ("Young Black Americans and the Criminal Justice System: Five Years Later"). It found that one in three (32.2 percent) black men between the ages of 20 and 29 are caught up in the criminal-justice system: either in prison, on parole or probation, or being prosecuted. And in some inner cities, the figure is one in two. Between 1989 and 1994, black women experienced the greatest increase (78 percent) in being placed under the criminal justice system of all demographic (human population) groups. And a major reason for involvement in the criminal justice system is drugs. The comparative figures between blacks and whites for drug violations in the criminal justice system are striking. A USA Today analysis of 1991 arrest data found:

- For all drug crime, blacks are arrested at a rate of about 1,600 for every 100,000 of the population. For whites, the rate is about 400 per 100,000.

- Blacks are arrested for the sale or manufacture of drugs at a rate of about 640 per 100,000; for whites, the rate is about 120 per 100,000.

- For possession, blacks are arrested at a rate of about 900 per 100,000; the rate for whites is about 270 per 100,000.

It is no accident that black people go through the criminal justice system in high proportions because law-enforcement authorities target them. For example, an African American who is driving along in a car with an out-of-state license is more likely than a white driver to be stopped by the police because he or she fits a profile of suspected drug traffickers. Steven B. Duke and Albert C. Gross report that a survey of car stoppings on the New Jersey Turnpike revealed that while only 4.7 percent of the cars were driven by blacks with out-of-state license plates, 80 percent of the drug arrests were made of blacks. Duke and Gross add: "In Memphis, about 75 percent of the air travelers stopped by drug police in 1989 were black, yet only 4 percent of the flying public is black."

The white majority in America are abusing drugs, just as African Americans and other minorities are. But the criminal justice system is more likely to penalize the racial minority than the racial majority. That is an injustice that destroys many lives in minority communities.

Police search this African American's car for drugs.

Crack. A Colombian drug cartel discovered that the introduction of crack would be a fine way to increase its marketing of illegal drugs in the United States. Because the price of cocaine hydrochloride was high and out of the financial reach of the poor, most African Americans were unaffected by its appeal. But crack was inexpensive and could be purchased for as little as $5, and sometimes even less than that. Thus, the low price of crack put this particular illegal substance in the financial range of people of limited economic means. To be sure, an overwhelming majority of African Americans do not take any illegal drugs, but the availability of cheap drugs had a severe impact among those who were poor and lived in inner cities.

Crack creates a short-term high at low cost, and that is its appeal. But the long-term consequences of taking crack could be financially disastrous, because the crack addict needs five times more crack than the cocaine addict needs powder cocaine to maintain his or her habit. The crack addict spends five times as much as the cocaine addict, according to a study of pharmacologists (those who study the changes produced in animals and people by drugs) at the University of California at Los Angeles.

Crack is damaging enough to African Americans, but the sentencing provisions for crack possession unfairly discriminate against them in an equally damaging way. Congress decided in the 1986 crime bill that crack was very dangerous and made the possession of five grams of crack in federal cases punishable by a mandatory (required) five-year sentence. A similar sentence involving powder cocaine requires possession of 500 grams, in other words, 100 times that amount.

Jefferson Morley, an assistant editor at the *Washington Post*, compared two drug dealers, one a supplier and one a street dealer. The supplier sells the street dealer three grams of cocaine. The street dealer mixes the drug with baking soda, cooks it in his microwave, and produces six grams of crack cocaine. "If he gets arrested and sent to federal court," Morley writes, "he faces a mandatory minimum of five years in jail. The supplier has to get caught with 500 grams of powder cocaine—about 1.7 pounds—to face that much time in federal prison."

The case against the unfairness of sentencing for crack is based on grounds of both science and the way in which the criminal justice system deals with crack offenders. As far as the science is concerned, it is important to keep in mind that crack is a form of cocaine, and in many respects there are few differences between the effect of powder cocaine and crack cocaine in producing similar physiological and psychoactive effects. Dorothy K. Hatsukami and Mariana W. Fischman of the psychiatry departments of the University of Minnesota and Columbia University respectively reported in an article in *The Journal of the American Medical Association* of November 20, 1996, that the physiological and psychoactive effects of cocaine hydrochloride and crack are nearly identical. But they found that the method used for taking the drugs produces different effects. Both intravenous use and smoking crack are more dangerous than snorting powder. The authors conclude that the 100 to 1 ratio is much too harsh and say that on the basis of science, the penalty should be 2 to 1 or 3 to 1.

People who argue that crack use deserves a very high penalty compared to that for powder cocaine say that crack causes greater violence and more health problems than powder cocaine. But science does not support that claim. In addition, they point to the damage that a pregnant woman who uses crack causes to her fetus (unborn young), who may be born with permanent physiological and psychological problems. It is true that a crack mother damages her fetus, but alcohol probably does even more damage. Yet we do not put people in prison for merely possessing alcohol. In addition, if American society were really concerned about the well-being of all babies, it would support more government programs to prevent birth defects. But it does not always do so to any significant degree. For example, the inability of some poor women to get state-funded prenatal (prior to birth) care causes more damage than crack.

What is surprising is that the widely accepted popular belief that crack is actually used more by black people than by white people is itself a myth. True, crack use is more prevalent within the black community than it is within the white community. But the percentage of African Americans in the entire U.S. population is considerably smaller than the percentage of whites. In terms of the absolute numbers of Americans who use crack, the white population makes up the largest share among racial categories. According to the U.S. Department of Health and Human Services *National Household Survey on Drug Abuse* in 1993, among those reporting crack use at least once in the previous year, 46 percent were white, 38 percent were black, and 10 percent were Hispanics. The total number of black users of crack is smaller than the total number of white crack users.

When it comes to the criminal justice system, however, there is an extraordinary imbalance in punishment that affects African Americans unfairly. Although more whites than blacks use crack, African Americans make up about 90 percent of those sentenced for crack crimes each year. The *Los Angeles Times* reported in 1995 that no white person has ever been convicted of a crack offense in the federal courts of Boston, Denver, Chicago, Los Angeles, Dallas, or Miami. Such patterns show that the law-enforcement authorities are applying the law in a way that causes unfair harm to African Americans.

Civil rights leader Jesse Jackson often speaks out against government policies that he believes are racist.

Some officials involved in government matters dealing with sentencing have tried to change the sentencing differences between the possession of crack and the possession of powder cocaine. For example, in the spring of 1995, the U.S. Sentencing Commission, a seven-member panel that monitors the federal prison system and makes recommendations to Congress, said that the ratio of 100 to 1 for crack/cocaine hydrochloride possession was too high and called for more flexibility in giving sentences. In the fall of 1995, however, the House and Senate voted to reject the commission's recommendation, so the 100 to 1 ratio remains in effect. In 1997, the Sentencing Commission proposed a more moderate reform that would reduce the disparity in sentencing. Congress was considering the new proposal.

It would be difficult to fault the criticisms of so many African-American leaders who have called for change. Civil rights leader Jesse Jackson expressed the view of many black people when he said of the crack/powder cocaine sentencing difference that "[it's] wrong; it's immoral; it's unfair; it's racist; it's ungodly." And Keith W. Watters, a past president of the National Bar Association, the country's largest black lawyers' organization, observes: "The [sentencing] system is so skewed [biased] against us that the law is losing its credibility as a neutral vehicle for fairness and equality in our society."

Government policy. Drug policies are racially discriminatory because of government policy in both domestic and foreign policy matters. In domestic matters, government has not done enough to provide economic opportunity to minorities, which would give them a chance for financial security. Drugs would play a less significant role in minority areas if decent jobs were available to the residents of those areas. But members of minorities often lack economic opportunities.

In the past, people with little formal education could move up the economic ladder as a result of hard work. The economy could use unskilled labor in its industrial system. But because of changes in the economy and advances in electronics, computers, and technology, the modern economy rewards people with advanced degrees and professional expertise rather than unskilled workers. The opportunities for many youngsters in the inner cities are now quite limited. Some minority teenagers discover that they cannot make a decent living working for minimum wage in some menial job as, say, a worker in a fast-food restaurant. Instead, they look elsewhere to earn money. And one of the areas that some of them consider is drug dealing. They see a possibility of earning hundreds of dollars each day. Most of the youngsters involved in illegal drugs, however, do not make large amounts of money. Instead, many become involved in gang wars or police raids. If they do not get killed or addicted, they may spend many years in prison.

It is not only the failure of government to provide good jobs that contributes to the plight of minorities in drug matters. It is also the specific policies that the government follows. In this regard, many African Americans are suspicious about the circumstances in which drugs come into their neighborhoods. They note that when African Americans became politically active as a result of the civil rights and Black Power movements of the 1960s, which called for fairer treatment for black Americans, huge quantities of drugs suddenly appeared in black communities. Some people within the black community believe that members of the white power structure (people in the community who are politically powerful) conspired to use drugs as a weapon to destroy black and Latino political activism that was challenging the existing power structure. These African Americans reason that a community that is drenched in drugs is in no physical or mental condition to challenge the white power structure. Louis Farrakhan, head of the Nation of Islam (a black nationalist organization), expresses the views of many people in the black community when he says: "The epidemic of drugs and violence in the black community stems from a calculated attempt by whites to foster black self-destruction."

Louis Farrakhan accused the white power structure of purposefully infiltrating the black community with drugs.

In its foreign policy, too, the United States contributed to the problem of drugs in African-American communities. After World War II, the United States was engaged in the cold war with the Soviet Union. (See Chapter 3.) Whenever there was a conflict between focusing on the cold war or on drugs, the United States sacrificed the latter for the former. But drugs did not ignore the United States, and they had a particularly devastating impact on inner cities, as the experience of U.S. involvement in Central America shows. In August 1996, the *San Jose Mercury* published three stories describing U.S. associations with the contras, a group of anticommunist Nicaraguans who were fighting the Sandinista government in Nicaragua. The United States viewed the Sandinista government as an enemy. The newspaper stories reported that two men gave money to the contras and at times met with contra leaders working with the CIA, a national-security unit, in the early 1980s. Some of these contras were responsible for the shipping of huge amounts of cheap cocaine into African-American communities in Los Angeles. The result was an epidemic of crack addiction that had a severe impact on African Americans. The articles did not specifically state that the CIA was directly involved but hinted that it was so.

Whatever the extent of government involvement in this matter, however, there is no question that in the 1980s, the United States supported contra groups, some of whom engaged in drug trafficking. A Senate Foreign

Relations subcommittee concluded in a 1989 report that drug smugglers were hired to move contra supplies and that "individual contras accepted weapons, money and equipment from drug smugglers." The subcommittee report, like the newspaper articles, does not specifically say that the CIA was involved, but it does state: "There are serious questions as to whether or not U.S. officials involved in Central America failed to address the drug issue for fear of jeopardizing the war effort against Nicaragua."

There are many other examples in which the United States ignored world trafficking in drugs because of reasons of national security. (See Chapter 3.) But the contra case shows what a devastating impact that crack cocaine had on the African-American community in Los Angeles.

Racial minorities have been hard hit as a result of drug policy in America. Because of the U.S. government's deliberate policies of neglect for minorities, the enactment of specific drug laws on crack, and the particular way that the government enforced drug laws against minorities, the government is much to blame for the harm that minorities experienced. With their lack of concern about the worldwide impact of drugs on American society, the decision makers who made U.S. foreign policy contributed to the plight of racial minorities in dealing with drugs.

NO. Federal, state, and local governments have passed laws and adopted policies to protect the public against the evils of drugs. That is the only purpose of those laws and policies. It is surprising that some people argue that the government is using the drug war to discriminate against minorities, because it is precisely minorities who are most hurt by the evils of drugs and are in need of the greatest protection. These evils are high crime, gang wars, killings, and illness. Drug laws and policies work to benefit minorities rather than to hurt them. It is wrong to consider the criminal justice system, crack sentencing, or U.S. foreign policy as doing anything to hurt racial minorities.

Criminal justice system. Far from acting in a discriminatory manner, the criminal justice system works effectively to help minority communities that are hard hit by drugs. The use of statistics of arrests and incarceration to prove racism is misleading because it does not take into account the reasons for the statistical differences between people of different races. There are sound reasons that explain why the statistics show a high percentage of minority members in trouble because of the drug laws.

First, minority communities are flooded with drugs. Most people in these communities do not take or deal with drugs but, rather, are victims of the dealers and users of drugs. John Jacob, president of the Urban League, a civil rights organization, expressed the views of civil rights leaders when he said: "Drugs kill more blacks than the [Ku Klux] Klan [a racist organization] ever did. They're destroying more children and more families than poverty ever did." And African-American people understand the danger since they are in the frontline of the drug battle. The police say that they receive so many complaints of drug deals and gangs in minority communities that they cannot cope with them all. But police make arrests in these communities because the communities demand it. If people in upscale white communities were to be faced with the same kind of gang violence that exists in the inner cities, they would be demanding that the police make more arrests in their communities, too.

Second, drug violations in minority communities are conducted more in the open than they are in the white communities. Police Chief John Dale of

Police bust drug dealers in a minority community.

Albany, New York, says, "We don't have whites on corners selling drugs.... They're in houses and offices."

It is not surprising, then, that in Albany, blacks are eight times as likely as whites to be arrested for drugs. In Albany as in many other cities, it is easier for the police to spot the drug dealing in the inner cities than in less easily detected areas, such as in homes and businesses in white neighborhoods.

Crack. The high penalty for crack is justified because of the consequences that this particular drug produces. Crack is associated with crimes against young and disadvantaged people who need protection against drug dealers and gangs who trade in this horrible substance. Crack is more dangerous in causing crime because it has a greater likelihood of being associated with violence, in part because crack dealers have more extensive criminal records than other drug dealers. Crack also produces dreadful health consequences that deserve special attention.

Some members of the Black Caucus, the African-American members of the House of Representatives

If crack sentencing is racist, then one could assume that the elected officials coming from districts that have large minority constituencies would have opposed writing such heavy penalties for crack into law. But that is not the case. The provision in the 1986 Anti-Drug Abuse Act dealing with penalties for crack possession had the support of 11 of the then 20 members of the Black Caucus, the African-American members of the House of Representatives. Charles Rangel, the chairman of the House Select Committee on Narcotics Abuse and Control, represents Harlem, a predominantly African-American district in Manhattan. He favored the strong measures against crack, saying that "crack was the newest and most insidious addition to the drug culture... cheaper than cocaine and more addictive."

Most minority members of Congress well understand that it is the minorities that suffer most from the drug scene. Because crack is so dangerous, severely punishing African Americans who do crack can only benefit the overwhelming majority of African Americans. The overwhelming majority of African Americans do not use crack. They are the victims of people who are crack addicts. By sentencing crack users to long terms, the criminal justice system removes from the African-American community people who will become drug dealers, engage in violent activity, and steal property—mostly of innocent African Americans who live in the same community.

It is true that blacks are arrested more than white people for crack crimes, but that does not come about because of racial prejudice. Rather, it comes about for two other reasons. First, people who live in the inner cities are mostly minorities. It is they who make the most police complaints because crack distribution in those communities is set in an environment of criminal behavior. Second, the nature of the crack-distribution trade affects the racial differences in arrests. Robert S. Litt, the deputy assistant attorney general for the Criminal Division of the Department of Justice, said that the disproportionate prosecution of blacks on crack offenses occurs because "[b]lacks dominate the crack distribution trade. The reasons blacks are getting arrested for distribution of crack is that blacks distribute crack."

More attention is given to the principle of crack sentences than the reality. When one looks at actual numbers of people who are affected by the crack sentencing, one can see that they are not really high. Writer Craig Horowitz notes in an article in New York magazine: "There were only 3,400 people convicted under the federal crack guidelines in 1994, and the overwhelming majority of them were hardened criminals or serious offenders. Only 51 were convicted after being arrested with only a small amount of crack, no previous record, and no weapon."

The criminal justice system, then, is fair. To the extent that harsh crack sentencing takes the most hardened criminals off the street in the inner cities, the safety of honest law-abiding minorities is strengthened.

Finally, crack causes dreadful and long-lasting health problems. The worst health damage, perhaps, is the damage that pregnant women who are addicted to crack cause when they give birth to their babies. Many of these babies are born premature and with small heads. They often need a lifetime of care. Society must do whatever is necessary to punish the dealers and users who are responsible for victimizing innocent children.

Government policy. Minority members have suffered from drugs, but it is not because government is responsible for their plight. Government policy has done much to improve education, enact civil rights laws, and adopt policies that assist racial minorities. The fact that so many minority members have achieved economic success and found a high place in American society shows that government is the friend, rather than the enemy, of minorities.

It is true that African Americans today are often treated poorly by white people and that they have less money than whites, too. But many black Americans have entered the professions and have achieved success in industry and other sectors of American society. African Americans were subject to worse treatment and were poorer a century or two ago than they are today, but they did not turn to drugs then. Cecil Williams, a black minister in San Francisco, says about cocaine what can be said about other drugs, as well: "Cocaine is foreign to African-American culture. We did not create it; we did not produce it; we did not ask for it." A society that today is far more responsive to minorities than it has ever been cannot be blamed for the drug problems of the inner cities.

The charge that the white power structure is responsible for the introduction of drugs into the African-American community lacks credibility. Drugs began coming into the United States in large quantities in the 1960s and affected members of every racial and economic group in American society. And they continue to do so. Students at predominantly white preparatory schools and universities use drugs, and some of them sell drugs for profit, as well. Wall Street stock and bond dealers use drugs as do people who live in rich and middle-class neighborhoods. All over America, drugs are in small towns as well as inner cities. And those who profit from the illegal sale of drugs come from different ethnic and racial groups. It is inaccurate to blame the white power structure for the problems of drugs in minority communities. It is foolish, too. If the white power structure were replaced by another racial group, there would still be drug problems in all communities. And if we are serious about controlling

Drugs are in small towns as well as inner cities.

drugs, we have to deal with real facts and not imagined conspiracies based on racial myths.

The charges made against the United States for the conduct of its foreign policy are simplistic and often false. It is true that the defining goal of the United States in its foreign policy during the cold war was to maintain U.S. national security and a democratic way of life. After pursuing this cold-war policy for nearly a half century, the Soviet Union collapsed and split into 15 independent countries. Communist governments elsewhere collapsed also. The United States won the cold war. All Americans, regardless of their racial background, benefited from that victory because Americans no longer faced a threat from a powerful Communist country. That the United States should have done more about drugs is probably true, but it could only do what was possible given the nature of international politics during the cold war.

As far as the specific charges about the contras, the CIA, and drugs are concerned, there is no evidence to support them. The CIA and Justice Department began investigations into the charges and concluded that the CIA was not responsible for the crack epidemic of the 1980s. The *Washington Post*, *Los Angeles Times*, and *New York Times* conducted their own investigations and challenged the conclusions of the *San Jose Mercury*'s articles. The *Washington Post*, for example, found no evidence that the CIA-backed contras—or Nicaraguans in general—played a major role in the emergence of crack as a narcotic in widespread use across the United States. Instead, it found that drug traffickers from many countries were responsible. According to the *Washington Post*'s analysis of widely accepted evidence from government reports and academic studies, although Nicaraguans took part in the cocaine trade at that time, "most of the cocaine trade was in the hands of Colombian and Mexican smugglers and distributors within the United States including Jamaicans, Dominicans, Haitians, and Americans of varying backgrounds."

No one would deny that drugs have had a devastating impact on the communities of African Americans and other racial groups. But government racist drug policies are not the reasons for the problem. Instead, factors such as the lure of high profits, the willingness of government officials to become corrupt, the availability of drugs, and the demand for drugs, are the reasons why drugs are such a problem not only for minorities but for all Americans.

Chapter 7
DRUG TESTING

Debate: Is There Too Much Drug Testing in the United States?

On December 3, 1996, the National Football League (NFL) suspended without pay tackle Leon Lett, the Dallas Cowboys' best defensive lineman, for a minimum of one year. According to the *Dallas Morning News*, Lett had tested positive for cocaine. Although Lett challenged the accuracy of the test, NFL Commissioner Paul Tagliabue turned down his appeal. "I am fully satisfied that the program's test collection and processing arrangements, to which the NFL and the NFL Players Association have agreed, fully ensure the integrity and accuracy of test results," Tagliabue said.

Lett's suspension was not an isolated event either for him or for his team. The NFL had suspended him for four games in the previous season for violation of the league's drug policy. And his new drug use was the sixth Dallas Cowboys' drug violation in the last two seasons. The League suspension of Lett could not have come as a surprise to him because the NFL's rules for drug use are clear. A player who tests positive a first time is required to take ten drug tests monthly. If he tests positive a second time, he can be suspended for a minimum of one year, during which time he may not participate with his team in any way.

Athletes who use drugs often do so because they believe that they will gain professionally by their use. Some athletes use stimulants to increase their competitiveness and make them more aggressive. They

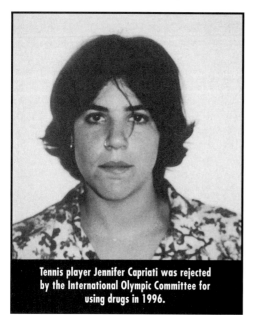
Tennis player Jennifer Capriati was rejected by the International Olympic Committee for using drugs in 1996.

take analgesics to reduce pain from injuries. They rely on steroids to enhance muscle development. But stimulants, analgesics, and steroids are banned substances in sports. Athletes know well enough that drugs can harm health and even kill as a result of dehydration (the loss of water from the body), over-heating, and heart and liver failure. Young people who use steroids may develop impairment (damage or loss of effectiveness) in their growth and sexual development.

Drug testing for athletes is a common practice not only in football but in other sports, such as basketball and baseball, as well. Both professional and collegiate athletes are often required to take tests. The International Olympic Committee has been conducting drug tests of Olympic contestants since 1968. Players have not only been suspended from participating in team activities, as the example of Lett shows, but they have in some cases been penalized by losing the prizes they earned. Even high school athletes are tested for drugs.

Athletes are not the only people who take drug tests. Federal government workers and employees in many private industries take drug tests. In all, about 50,000 federal government employees are tested every year. The military requires drug testing. Employees in federal agencies involved in sensitive or safety work, such as the FBI, DEA, INS, and the Federal Aviation Administration, are required to take tests. Many states have enacted legislation that follows the features of testing programs used by the federal government. A law enacted in 1990 by the state of Georgia even required candidates for Georgia's high state electoral offices to pass drug tests before they could get on a ballot. (In 1997, however, the U.S. Supreme Court struck down the

Georgia law on constitutional grounds.) Police in many cities must take drug tests, too.

Many companies require job applicants to undergo drug tests. Among these companies are Exxon, IBM, Federal Express, AT&T, and some Wall Street financial institutions. Smaller companies, however, are less likely to use drug tests than are larger companies. The U.S. Department of Labor's Bureau of Labor Statistics reports that only 3 percent of small businesses have drug-testing programs, and only 12 percent have a formal policy on drug use. But in larger companies—those with 250 or more employees—46 percent of employers test their workers, and 74 percent have formal antidrug policies.

The movement for drug tests had its origins in the armed services when DOD started a program in 1970 to identify drug abusers—particularly those returning from the Vietnam War who were addicted to heroin. The purpose of the program was to give the members of the armed forces treatment before coming home. The military continued to have drug problems. A DOD survey in 1980 discovered that nearly half the younger people in the military were using marijuana. As a result, each service began a drug-detection program. In 1981, an accident aboard the aircraft carrier USS *Nimitz* revealed widespread drug use among sailors.

In 1986, President Ronald Reagan issued a directive (executive order) setting up a policy for drug testing of U.S. government employees under certain conditions. In addition to testing when an individual agrees to voluntarily submit to drug testing, the Reagan directive provided that the federal government can use drug tests of federal workers under any of the following conditions:

(1) When there is a reasonable suspicion that any employee uses illegal drugs.

(2) In an examination authorized by the agency regarding an accident or unsafe practice.

(3) As part of or as a follow-up to counseling or rehabilitation for illegal drug use through an employee assistance program (a program that helps employees with drug or alcohol problems).

In 1988, Congress followed up the directive by enacting the Drug Free Workplace Act of 1988. It requires all persons obtaining federal contracts worth more than $25,000 for performing work or providing services to any federal government agency to maintain a drug-free work environment. The law, however, does not make drug testing a legal requirement.

To carry out government and private policy on drug abuse, laboratories use a variety of tests, including the testing of blood, saliva, and hair, and even the use of brain scans. But the most common test is urinalysis (a urine test), a procedure employed for many purposes in medical analyses. A urine test can detect the presence of illegal drugs in the body.

The kind of test chosen depends on what the investigator is looking for. Hair analysis can detect long-term use. One report shows that an analysis of a 5-inch (13-cm) strand of hair can give a month-by-month record of cocaine or other drug use reaching back nearly a year. The hair test will detect heroin, PCP, or cocaine used within the previous three months. But marijuana and cocaine cannot be detected in recent use through hair analysis because several days are needed for these drugs to be deposited in the hair. Urinalysis is short-term and can detect the presence of drugs taken within the past few hours or days. Recent drug use is best detected by urinalysis.

The idea of testing is based on the fact that when substances are taken into the body, whether through eating, smoking, or injection, they undergo chemical changes in the body. The substances that are not absorbed are eliminated as body wastes. This changing composition of chemicals is known as metabolism. Urine testing can detect the presence of such metabolites (the organic compounds produced by metabolism). But some drugs are metabolized more quickly than others. Cocaine is metabolized quickly, but marijuana can remain in the body for weeks.

Because first-round tests are not reliable, accuracy in determining the presence of drugs requires follow-up tests that use a different method of analysis than the first test. These tests are more costly and require more laboratory time than the first-round tests, but they are capable of identifying illegal drugs with more accuracy than the first-round tests. The best confirming test is called gas chromatography/mass spectrometry, or GC/MS. It makes a positive identification by breaking down drugs into their molecules (the smallest particles of a substance).

Both because of expense and as a matter of policy, the kinds of drug tests given differ from place to place. Most workplace tests fall into six categories: preemployment, reasonable suspicion, postaccident, posttreatment, random testing, and voluntary. Preemployment tests are given to people applying for jobs. People who demonstrate odd behavior, such as mood swings, absenteeism, and frequent lateness, may demonstrate reasonable suspicion of drug use. An employee involved in an accident (such as a pilot who crashes his or her plane) is subject to automatic drug testing. Posttreatment involves people who return from treatment or rehabilitation (recovery) from drug use. Random testing is unannounced testing by an organization of individuals without any direct indication that the individuals have taken drugs. Voluntary tests are given to individuals, such as supervisors, who wish to set an example for others.

Drug tests have become commonplace in the United States. They seem to be used in more and more situations. In 1996, for example, the state of Maryland was considering extending drug tests to welfare beneficiaries. If the Maryland legislature succeeds in passing such a law, Maryland would deny welfare benefits to anyone on welfare in the state who tests positive for drugs. Those testing positive would be offered treatment for drug abuse. The purpose of such a move is to prevent welfare recipients who are hooked on drugs to use welfare money to feed their drug habit rather than to meet their legitimate needs, such as paying rent or buying food.

The widespread use of drug tests has raised questions about what they achieve and the methods in which they are employed. Challenges to the use of the drug tests are continually being made in the workplace and in the courts.

DEBATED:

IS THERE TOO MUCH DRUG TESTING IN THE UNITED STATES?

Yes. In principle, drug tests serve a noble purpose: to determine whether individuals take illegal drugs. They also help determine whether individuals responsible for public safety and national security are living drug-free lives. In practice, however, drug testing is used far more than is necessary because the limitations of drug testing are too often overlooked. These limitations are based on testing errors and consequences to society. In addition, there are better alternatives to dealing with drug problems than relying on drug tests.

Errors. In principle, a perfect system of drug testing may be devised. In reality, however, drug testing produces many errors. Errors may take different forms. A false-positive is the finding by a drug test of a drug that is not, in fact, present in the tested sample. A false-negative is the failure of a test to find a drug that is, in fact, in the tested sample. A misidentification is finding a drug in a drug test but identifying it mistakenly. Experience with evaluating drug tests shows that there are specimen mix-ups, erroneous false-positives, and direct observation problems.

Tests can falsely show positive for illegal drugs when in fact a person has consumed legal products. For example, poppy seeds, which are found in some rolls and bagels, give a positive reading for opiates. Over-the-counter drugs, such as Ibuprofen, Alka Seltzer, and cold medicines, can also cause positive test results. Even taco grease sometimes indicates positive drug use.

Sometimes, an error is detected. For example, the International Olympic Committee in Seoul, Korea, prematurely announced that British runner Linford Christie had failed a drug test only to reverse itself and let him keep his silver medal when it found that the banned substance in his urine came from ginseng tea. Some individuals testing positive for drugs are not so fortunate as Linford Christie, however, and suffer penalties because they are falsely accused of taking drugs. All some tests show is that a person came into contact with some drug at some time. But tests may not give sufficient information to indicate the way that the drug got into a person's body or whether it was by legal or illegal means. Being in a room with people who smoke marijuana may leave traces in the blood of a person who is in the same room even if that person is a nonuser of marijuana.

The International Olympic Committee prematurely announced that British runner Linford Christie had failed a drug test, when in fact he had passed the test.

Errors are not uncommon in laboratories. The National Institute of Drug Abuse (NIDA) certifies some laboratories, but it does not certify them all. Some companies use labs that are not certified, and their results are thought to be more error-prone than certified labs. There is much evidence of lab error. The Centers for Disease Control, an agency of the U.S. Public Health Service, conducted studies of the reliability of urine testing from 1972 to 1981. The centers concluded that some methods of drug testing were better than others, but none was 100 percent accurate. In a 1985 study, the centers found the error rate for amphetamine tests ranged from 19 percent to 100 percent, and from cocaine tests, the error rate ranged from zero percent to 100 percent.

In late 1990 and early 1991, three out of 63 labs certified by NIDA in the United States were suspended for documented cases of false-positives. In 1992, an inspector general's audit of the Interior Department's employee drug-testing program uncovered widespread evidence of mismanagement, including inaccurate reporting of test results, mishandling of urine specimens, destruction of records, and possible advance notification of employees to be tested. The entire Department of the Interior's drug-testing program from January 1, 1989 to August 1992 was thrown out after the department's inspector general declared it unreliable. The inspector general found that 37 people who tested positive were not illegal drug users, and 61 samples that were not tested were reported as negative.

It is not enough to say that tests are generally accurate, because the number of people harmed by false reports of drug use may be considerable. A test that is 95 percent accurate produces 50,000 false-positives when a million specimens are tested. The 50,000 people affected by the tests may protest, but there is no guarantee for many of them that their protests will be given the attention and consideration that they deserve.

Finally, clever people can beat the system. Success at detection through urine tests depends on several factors: the amount of drugs consumed, the time since the drug was taken, individual metabolic rates, the type of drug, and the amount of water consumed before collecting the urine specimen. To beat a test and get a false-negative, an individual may consume large quantities of water, use diuretics (drugs that increase the rate of urine formation by the kidneys), or adulterate (contaminate) the urine with salt or ammonia. A person can also substitute someone else's urine.

Consequences to society. It is true that tests may detect illegal substances, but much of the search for illegal drugs does not take into account the real problems of drugs in the workplace. A person may be on legal drugs and pass the drug test. But he or she may be more impaired from a legal substance, such as a medication prescribed by a doctor, than from an illicit substance.

In addition, most companies do not test for alcohol impairment. But alcohol has caused the greatest damage in the workplace—greater than that caused by all illegal drugs combined. And there is evidence that the knowledge that they will be required to take drug tests will lead some individuals to switch to alcohol. *The Army Times* reported that in the first two years of military testing, the percentage of servicemen using marijuana dropped from 38 percent to 25 percent. But after these two years, the percentage of enlisted men who reported that alcohol had affected their performance had increased from 27 percent to 34 percent.

There is, moreover, no assurance that drug tests will detect all drug abusers, and worker morale may be hurt when employees know that some people who use drugs avoid being caught. Because government agencies have flexibility in how they carry out regulations, there is no certainty that drug tests will catch the right people. A security guard at one facility may be tested many times, whereas a security guard at a similar establishment elsewhere may not get tested at all. In addition, even when drug tests are accurate, they may miss the more serious drug abusers. Because cocaine leaves the system after two or three days and marijuana lingers on for weeks or months, drug testing punishes casual marijuana users. But workers with heavy cocaine and alcohol abuse habits may go undetected and cause more damage to an organization than marijuana users. Even when tests show positive, they do not provide enough information. Accidents in the workplace are most likely to be caused by heavy users, but tests cannot distinguish heavy users from recreational (casual) users.

One may also wonder about the consequences of drug testing outside of the workplace. If individuals are fired from their jobs, they may be more likely to resort to crime to obtain the money they need to feed their habit. From a societal point of view, then, an unemployed individual may cause more harm to others by being unemployed than by having a mild addiction.

Finally, the drug-testing program is not cost effective. Estimates of the cost of drug tests reach over $100 million per year. But in some sectors of society, there really is no drug problem of any significance. The federal government is a case in point. Between 0.5 and 1 percent of all federal employees have tested positive, and 90 percent of those who test positive are found to have consumed cannabis. A House subcommittee on the Civil Service reports that on the basis of screening 38 federal agencies, the government had to spend $77,000 in tests in order to find one person who tested positive. That is a lot of money to deal with so inconsequential a problem.

Alternatives. Drug tests are really not needed when alternatives exist that can achieve the same goals. A good supervisor can evaluate job performance without the use of a drug test. For example, a supervisor does not need to be a Ph.D. in business management to know that a worker who is late, sloppy, or subject to mood swings is acting suspiciously. A boss or supervisor should evaluate a worker solely on job performance. It is not fair to fire or penalize employees for what they did on Saturday night so long as when they come in for work on Monday, their performance has not been affected. Companies, then, can provide supervisors with better training to detect performance problems than they currently receive.

In addition to better supervision, organizations can rely on educational programs that furnish information about the dangers of drug use. People are influenced by such educational campaigns. It was such a campaign that was responsible for the reduction in the percentage of Americans using tobacco and alcohol in the past few decades. (See p. 59.)

Finally, instead of requiring drug tests, other tests to measure performance rather than evaluating personal behavior can be used. They do not require individuals to be observed as they urinate. An example of performance testing is a video game-playing program that tests an individual's ability to perform mental and physical tasks. A performance test measures how well an employee functions in the workplace on a particular day. No personal information is required.

The United States has the legitimate and noble goal of reducing drug use. But the use of tests to achieve this goal has gone too far. Drug tests are subject to too many errors. They produce more harmful consequences to society when their objectives can be achieved in better ways.

No. Drug tests serve so many useful purposes that they should not only be continued, but also should be increased in number and scope. Use of drug tests for welfare recipients, for example, may achieve some positive benefits in detecting whether welfare benefits are being used for purchasing drugs.

Errors. The case against drug testing based on the argument that drug tests are inaccurate is unfair. Of course, there are errors in drug testing as there are in every human effort. Heart surgeons make errors, too, but that is not a case against doctors performing surgery for victims of heart disease. The quality of drug tests has improved since the early 1970s, and NIDA certification of labs encourages those labs that rely on that certification to maintain high standards. False-positives can be eliminated with quality control. In general, testing is accurate if one uses good labs, watches specimens carefully, and does follow-up tests.

Current methods of drug testing assure a high rate of accuracy. Standard practice requires that when a first test is positive, a follow-up test relying on a different method of analysis be used. The result is that the analysis is highly accurate. People who test positive for drugs often complain about the accuracy of the tests because they look for any means to prevent detection. Lying is one of those means. One should not be deceived by the complaints of drug users that they are innocent. Often, the same person will test positively in other drug tests, thus leading objective observers to be skeptical about the initial protests of innocence.

Finally, it is not so easy to beat the system. Testing procedures have become perfected over the past few decades. Laboratories have put in place methods that can detect fraud so as to minimize deceitful activity. The fact that so many attempts to fool the system have been detected shows that the drug-testing procedures are working well.

Consequences to society. Drug tests serve many useful purposes. First, they serve as a deterrent (a means of discouragement) to the use of illegal drugs. Studies in 1991 conducted by the U.S. Department of Health and Human Services show that in any particular year about 7 percent of U.S. workers use an illicit drug and that approximately two-thirds of all illicit drug users are employed full time. The workplace, consequently, is an excellent location to make extraordinary efforts to stop drugs, and workplace drug tests are an effective instrument in the war against drugs. Thanks to the Reagan executive order of 1986 and subsequent government regulations, fewer than 1 percent of federal employees test positive for drug use.

A person with a good job wants to keep that job. If the person knows that he or she may be required to take a drug test, then that person is less likely to take illegal drugs than a person who works at a company or organization that does not require such tests. Regardless of whether or not the person's efficiency on the job would be impaired through drug use, he or she would probably think twice before taking drugs even for recreational

The goal of modern drug-testing procedures is to eliminate error.

purposes on a weekend or holiday, lest evidence of such drug taking show up on a test days, weeks, or even months later. As a case in point, when Pfizer, Inc., the New York-based pharmaceutical company, began testing job applicants in 1987, 9.9 percent showed evidence of recent drug use. By 1992, however, the percentage had dropped to 3.2 percent. In addition, after the Navy started testing Navy personnel for drugs, drug use declined. Drug use has gone down in the workplace as a result of drug tests generally.

Drug tests for people engaged in work for government and private organizations, consequently, offer a benefit going beyond performance on the job. That benefit involves leading a healthier, safer, and better life for the individual and his or her family members.

Athletes benefit from drug tests, too, because the tests discourage drug use. Drugs can give athletes an unfair competitive advantage. If some athletes took drugs to give them that competitive advantage, the practice would encourage other athletes to take drugs. Not only adult professional athletes but even high school athletes who aspire to a career in professional sports would feel the pressure to do so. The taking of these drugs, however, may lead to serious health problems and possibly premature death.

Drug tests can prevent people from taking drugs in the same sense that enforcement of drunk-driving laws can affect the behavior of people who drive cars. If it is known that police are enforcing drunk-driving laws, a person who plans to attend a party at which alcoholic beverages will be served will be more likely to either not drink alcohol at all at the party, choose a designated driver, or use public transportation to get to and from the party than if no drunk-driving laws existed. Drug tests like drunk-driving laws, then, save lives.

Many employers are more concerned about what happens at work than about the impact of any given policy on society in general. Drug testing produces great benefits in the workplace. Because drug tests result in a decline in drug use, the number of accidents in the workplace declines. Sometimes these accidents are deadly. In January 1987, for example, a Conrail freight train ran a stop signal and slid into the path of an Amtrak passenger train, killing 16 people and injuring 175. Both crewmen of the freight train had marijuana in their system at the time of the accident. The law now specifically requires drug testing for people involved in key aspects of transportation. Airplane pilots, truck drivers, and train operators, for example, are subject to periodic drug tests. And these tests have been responsible for preventing the kind of transportation accident that befell the hapless victims of the Conrail incident.

Two crewmen of the Conrail freight train involved in a 1987 accident had marijuana in their system at the time of the accident.

But there are many other jobs in which accidents could occur that would endanger the lives of fellow workers, customers, and even innocent bystanders. A drug-influenced janitor may be careless with cleaning fluids and cause a fire, resulting in possible deaths, injuries, and property destruction. A drug-taking worker in a construction company may endanger the lives of fellow workers because of inattention to simple safety measures.

In addition to improved safety, a drug-free workplace is likely to produce less absenteeism than a workplace that is not drug-free. In a study of the U.S. Postal Service in the late 1980s, for example, 5,465 job applicants were tested for use of illicit drugs. Tests made after an average of 1.3 years of employment showed that employees who tested positive for illicit drugs had an absenteeism rate of 59.3 percent higher than employees who had tested negative. Employees who had tested positive also had a 47 percent higher rate of involuntary turnover (being fired or forced to resign) than employees who had tested negative. Studies of U.S. workers in general show that employees with a drinking or drug problem are absent three times more often than drug-free employees.

Companies rise or fall for many reasons, but the quality of the workforce is one vital part of a company's success. If a person is absent from work, then that absence may affect the efficiency of the work product. Colleagues who relied on the person to complete his or her work will now have to wait until the person returns. And a replacement worker is not likely to have the experience that the absent worker has. A company is bound to lose as a result of absenteeism. The taking of drugs is a factor in worker absenteeism. To the extent that drug tests reduce drug use by employees, the worker-absentee rate will be low.

It is sometimes said that drug tests reduce worker morale because the tests are a signal to employees that management does not trust them. But the truth is that drug tests at the workplace are a morale booster for employees. Most employees approve of drug tests. They do not want to be working with people stoned (high) on drugs. So long as employers explain to their employees why they are engaged in testing and why they are spending so much money for this effort, they are likely to get a positive employee response. As is often the case, particularly in large organizations, it helps when the organization is willing to offer an employee assistance program for the purpose of rehabilitation.

So many benefits result from a drug-free workplace in addition to low absenteeism, greater safety, and increased productivity that it is surprising that opponents of drug testing refer to the practice as anti-employee or pro-management. When workplace productivity increases, a company is more competitive and is likely to earn higher profits, create more jobs, and pay higher salaries. Health-insurance rates are likely to be less, too, as employees not on drugs will have fewer medical problems. Management and employees both gain from a drug-free workplace, which drug testing helps produce.

Finally, the benefits of drug testing are well worth the cost. One need think about the cost in lives and property of a single airplane crash caused by a drug-taking pilot to recognize the amount of damage that drugs can produce. The estimated $100 million per year spent on drug tests is nothing compared to the savings from increased productivity, decline in absenteeism, and better safety records.

Alternatives. Alternatives to drug tests have some value, but they cannot produce the kind of information that is needed to maintain a drug-free environment. Better training of supervisors to detect drug users will help organizations identify some offenders, but even such training is not good enough for supervisors to detect many individuals who are on drugs. Anti-drug educational programs are excellent, but they are not enough to stop or sharply reduce drug use.

Finally, the argument that the computer or other performance test that judges reflexes and general performance is an alternative is without merit. Performance tests measure hand-eye coordination, but not judgment or memory—features that are so vital in a workplace setting.

Drug tests have served legitimate purposes in the United States since they were first applied in the military in 1970. Although not perfect, they are highly accurate—particularly when proper procedures have been put in place to avoid errors. By putting pressure on people in the workplace, they have a far-ranging impact on American society—not only in the workplace but at home, as well. Drug tests work better than any other means to detect drug use. The courts have carefully weighed and balanced drug tests with our system of rights and have properly upheld drug tests. Use of drug tests should not only continue but be applied in even more areas to control the evil of drugs, which is a threat to public health and safety.

Chapter 8

CONCLUSION: THE FUTURE OF DRUG-ABUSE POLICY

As the 20th century comes to an end, issues of drug-abuse policy in the United States continue to be debated. How they will be resolved will depend on many factors, including cultural developments, the quality of law enforcement, scientific achievements, evaluation of drug policies, financial resources, and developments in other countries.

At present, Americans overwhelmingly find that drugs are dangerous to health and society. However, changes in American culture can replace opposition to drug use to a celebration of drug use, as was the case for the counterculture in the 1960s and 1970s. (See Chapter 1.) Each generation decides for itself about the proper role of drugs in society. American society may also continue to be hostile to drug use but debate whether the decision to do drugs is appropriate for individuals to make on their own or for government to make on behalf of the American people.

To the extent that law-enforcement agencies get better at stopping the flow of drugs into the United States or smashing drug-distribution networks, the supply of drugs in the United States will decline. In the late 20th century, however, the flow of drugs continues into the United States in spite of successes in seizing some illegal drugs.

The flow of drugs continues into the United States in spite of successful seizures.

But the use of more sophisticated police technology and better coordination among law-enforcement agencies may make these agencies more effective in fighting the drug war.

Scientific investigators continue to research drugs. Asking questions about why some people become addicted will still guide research into drug abuse. So, too, will investigations of the treatments that work to cure addiction. These treatments may be pharmacological, or they may be more psychological in nature.

As with most public-policy issues in a democracy, Americans will evaluate existing drug policies. No doubt the debate will be influenced by individuals who are helped or hurt by existing drug policy, people who hold philosophical views about the appropriate role of government in society, and objective analysis of the facts. Key debates may center on decriminalization and on the likelihood of stopping the flow of drugs into the United States.

Since the 1970s, the American people have been willing to support the spending of huge sums at the national and state levels to fight drug abuse. Law enforcement has received a large amount of these funds. Some of the money has gone to pay for treatment, too. Willingness to continue to spend large amounts of money will depend, however, on the success of the economy and on a feeling that the money devoted to dealing with drugs will do some good in solving the drug problem.

And developments in drug policy will depend on factors outside of the United States. With so many countries involved in drugs—whether in growing plants, processing the plants in laboratories, providing precursor chemicals, serving as a transit country, or money laundering—it is impossible for the United States to ignore practices that go on beyond its borders. It can and has influenced developments in other countries. But will other countries respond to the demands of the United States in drug matters to a greater extent than they have in the past?

Even the staunchest critics of drug abuse understand that the United States will always have individuals who succumb to drugs. But they hope that the extent of drug abuse can be minimized as a result of individual choices as well as intelligent public policies. Those choices and policies can be sound when important issues about drug abuse are identified and debated, as befits a democracy.

ABBREVIATIONS

AID	Agency for International Development
AIDS	Acquired Immunodeficiency Syndrome
CIA	Central Intelligence Agency
DEA	Drug Enforcement Administration
DOD	Department of Defense
FBI	Federal Bureau of Investigation
HHS	Department of Health and Human Services
HIV	Human Immunodeficiency Virus
INS	Immigration and Naturalization Service
Interpol	International Criminal Police Organization
LSD	Lysergic acid diethylamide
NFL	National Football League
NIDA	National Institute of Drug Abuse
ONDCP	Office of National Drug Control Policy
OTA	Office of Technology Assessment
PCP	phencyclidine
RICO	Racketeer Influenced and Corrupt Organizations
SAMSHA	Substance Abuse & Mental Health Services Administration
THC	tetrahydrocannabinol

GLOSSARY

adulterate Contaminate.

AIDS (Acquired Immunodeficiency Syndrome) A disease that attacks the body's immune system and is usually fatal.

analgesic drugs Drugs used to relieve pain.

bail A sum of money given by, or on behalf of, an arrested person in exchange for his or her temporary release as security for that person's required appearance in court.

balloon principle When a finger is pressed at one point on a balloon, that point collapses, but the balloon expands at another point. The term is used to apply to the ability of drug dealers to find new locations in which to traffic in drugs after law-enforcement authorities have destroyed or damaged old locations.

bootleggers Those who make, sell, or transport for sale alcoholic liquor illegally.

cannabis The hemp plant, from which marijuana is derived.

carcinogen A cancer-causing substance.

cartel An alliance of independent business organizations formed to regulate production, pricing, and marketing of goods by its members.

cerebral hemorrhage Bleeding of the brain.

certification (U.S. drug policy) A process in which the President is required to assure that all drug-producing and/or drug-transit countries are "cooperating fully" with U.S. antidrug policies or have taken their own measures against drugs and financial wrongdoing with drug money.

cirrhosis A disease of the liver that results in liver failure and death.

civil liberties Individual rights under the law.

cocaine A drug made from the coca leaf. It is a stimulant that energizes its user.

cocaine hydrochloride Powder cocaine.

cold war A period of continuing conflict between the United States and the Soviet Union along economic, political, and ideological lines, which lasted for nearly a half century. It also involved for each of these countries the creation of a military force strong enough to deter an armed attack by the opposing side.

confiscate Seize by the government for the public treasury.

contraband Illegal imports.

Controlled Substances Act Enacted in 1970, this law brought together existing laws and regulations on drugs. It changed the system of penalties for drug violations and increased the regulation of medicinal drugs.

convulsions Abnormal muscle disturbances.

counterculture A movement of the 1960s that rejected traditional values and became rebellious against established society.

crack An inexpensive form of cocaine.

crack houses Dwellings for crack addicts who live in dirty and unhealthy surroundings.

czar Someone who has great authority in a particular area.

decriminalization of drugs The reduction of penalties for the use of drugs.

deforestation The clearing away of forests.

dependence A need to take a drug regularly to prevent either physiological or psychological symptoms.

depressants Drugs that depress the central nervous system, resulting in the reduction of stress and excitement and a decrease in bodily activity.

detoxification A treatment for drug abuse in which the body is cleansed of drugs.

diuretics Drugs that increase the rate of urine formation by the kidneys.

double jeopardy Putting someone on trial for an offense for which that person has already been put on trial.

drug abuse A condition in which a person takes a drug in a manner that harms that individual and may also harm others.

Drug Enforcement Administration (DEA) The federal agency charged with responsibility for enforcing federal drug laws.

drug paraphernalia Articles used to administer illegal drugs.

drug-transit countries Countries through which drugs pass on their way to countries in which those drugs are distributed.

due process Protection against the government's acting to deny an individual life, liberty, or property beyond what the law allows.

ephedrine A substance used in making methamphetamine.

eradication Destruction.

euphoria A feeling of great happiness.

extradition A method by which one country sends an accused criminal to another country that has the legal authority to try that individual.

false-negative The failure of a drug test to find a drug that is, in fact, in the tested sample.

false-positive The finding by a drug test of a drug that is not, in fact, present in the tested sample.

fetus Unborn young.

forfeiture A process in which money or property is surrendered.

freebase A method used to convert cocaine hydrochloride into crack.

gateway theory The theory that when individuals use a weak drug, such as marijuana, they go on to use more powerful drugs, like cocaine and heroin.

glaucoma An eye disease.

global warming The warming of the Earth's atmosphere by the release of carbon dioxide and other gases.

gross domestic product A nation's total output of goods and services.

Hague Opium Convention An international convention concluded in 1912 that called for controlling opiates and cocaine.

hallucinations False perceptions of reality; delusions.

hallucinogen A drug that affects perception, sensation, and emotion; also known as a psychedelic, a substance that causes hallucinations.

Harrison Narcotic Act A law enacted in 1914 that regulated traffic in narcotics and other drugs. It required doctors and pharmacists to keep records of drug distribution, and also required the purchase of tax stamps to ensure government supervision of drug sales.

hashish A preparation made from the *Cannabis sativa* hemp plant.

hepatitis A disease of the liver.

herbicide A substance that kills plants.

heroin A powerfully addictive narcotic that comes from morphine, sometimes called "dope" or "smack."

high A state of excitement, intoxication, or great happiness, often produced by a drug.

hippies People, usually young, who reject conventional behavior.

HIV (Human Immunodeficiency Virus) The virus that causes AIDS.

hypodermic syringe A medical instrument used to inject fluids into a body.

ideological Concerned with ideas.

imperialism The policy of a strong nation using its power to dominate a weak nation.

indictments Statements of criminal charges.

indigent Poor.

inhalants Legal products, like paint, glue, nail polish remover, and propane, that can be breathed in to get a high.

insomnia Inability to sleep.

interdiction Cutting off; forbidding.

intravenous Within the veins.

junkies Addicts.

legalization of drugs The elimination of laws that make it a crime to use or sell drugs.

litigants Persons engaged in a lawsuit.

LSD (lysergic acid diethylamide) A powerful synthetic drug, sometimes called "acid," which produces psychotic symptoms.

mainlining Injecting intravenously, usually an illegal drug.

marijuana A drug that comes from the dried leaves of the hemp plant.

Marijuana Tax Act A law passed in 1937 that placed a one-dollar tax per ounce of marijuana on anyone who grew, transported, sold, prescribed, or used marijuana. The law required everyone who did so to register.

metabolism The changing composition of chemicals within a living body.

metabolites The organic compounds produced by metabolism.

methadone A legally approved synthetic drug used to treat heroin addicts.

methamphetamine A synthetic drug that is a member of the amphetamine family and acts as a stimulant on the central nervous system.

middlemen Traders who buy from producers and sell to retailers or consumers.

migraine A severe headache.

misidentification In a drug test, finding a drug but identifying it mistakenly.

money laundering The conversion of money obtained through illegal means into money that appears to have come from a legal source in an attempt to avoid detection by government authorities.

morphine A narcotic that is made from the opium poppy.

multiple sclerosis A disease of the central nervous system.

narcotics Depressants that prevent a person from feeling pain. Some of the more popularly known narcotics are the opiates, such as morphine and heroin.

opiates Substances made from the opium poppy.

outpatient drug-free treatment A rehabilitation treatment in which addicts live in their own homes and make regular or occasional visits to a treatment source.

paranoia A tendency toward delusions, usually of persecution.

patent medicines Medicines that could be obtained without a prescription.

PCP (phencyclidine) A hallucinogen that is known as "angel dust."

peyote An organic hallucinogen.

pharmacological Pertaining to the use of drugs to deal with medical problems.

physiological Relating to the functioning of the body.

power structure People in the community who are politically powerful.

precursor chemicals Chemicals that can be used in processing illegal drugs.

Prohibition The barring of the sale of alcohol, as a result of the adoption of the Eighteenth Amendment to the Constitution and legislation enforcing that amendment.

psychoactive drugs Drugs that affect the mind and mental processes.

psychosis A severe mental disorder.

recidivism Return to criminal behavior.

rehabilitation Restoration to a state of health.

Rohypnol A drug that is used for treatment of severe insomnia. Often called the "date-rape" drug.

rush In connection with drugs, a feeling that is quick and powerful.

sanctions Penalties.

schedules Governmental lists of groups or categories of drugs subject to legal controls or restrictions.

search warrant A written order by a court that directs a law-enforcement official to search for a specific item in a particular place and to seize it if it is there.

skin-popping Injecting a drug under the skin.

snort Inhale.

speakeasy A place that illegally sold alcohol during Prohibition.

stimulants Drugs that make people feel more alert and excited, and reduce or remove tiredness. Stimulants include amphetamines, cocaine, caffeine, nicotine, and Ritalin.

straight One who does not depart from established acceptable behavior; one who does not use drugs.

therapeutic communities Long-term residential treatment centers that are designed for hard-core drug users who have not been successful with other treatment.

tolerance In connection with drugs, a state in which the body becomes less responsive to a specific drug and so has a need for increasing doses of that drug in order to get a high feeling.

tranquilizers Drugs that have a calming effect.

urinalysis A urine test employed for many purposes in medical analysis, frequently used to detect the presence of illegal drugs in the body.

waiver The intentional giving up of a right, claim, or privilege.

withdrawal A period during which an addict stops taking drugs, usually marked by nausea, chills, vomiting, muscular pains and cramps, and running nose.

BIBLIOGRAPHY

Chapter 1: Introduction: The Use of Drugs

Jonnes, Jill. *Hep-Cats, Narcs, and Pipe Dreams: A History of America's Romance with Illegal Drugs.* New York: Scribner, 1996.

Musto, David F. *The American Disease: Origins of Narcotic Control,* expanded edition. New York: Oxford University Press, 1987.

Woods, Geraldine. *Drug Abuse in Society: A Reference Handbook.* Santa Barbara, CA: ABC-Clio, 1993.

Chapter 2: Drugs of Abuse: A Portrait

Henderson, Leigh A., and William J. Glass, eds. *LSD: Still With Us After All These Years.* New York: Lexington Books, 1994.

Longenecker, Gesina L. *How Drugs Work: Drug Abuse and the Human Body.* Emeryville, CA: Ziff-Davis Press, 1994.

Stimmel, Barry, and the Editors of Consumer Reports Books. *The Facts About Drug Use: Coping with Drugs and Alcohol in Your Family, at Work, in Your Community.* New York: Haworth Press, 1993. (Originally published Yonkers, NY: Consumer Report Books, 1991.)

Williams, Terry. *Crack House: Notes from the End of the Line.* Reading, MA: Addison-Wesley Publishing Co., 1992.

Chapter 3: The War on Drugs

Baum, Dan. *Smoke and Mirrors: The War on Drugs and the Politics of Failure.* Boston, MA: Little, Brown, 1996.

Duke, Steven B., and Albert C. Gross. *America's Longest War: Rethinking Our Tragic Crusade Against Drugs.* New York: G.P. Putnam's Sons, 1993.

Office of National Drug Control Policy. *The National Drug Control Strategy: 1996.* Washington, D.C.: Office of National Drug Control Policy, 1996.

Payne, Douglas W. "Drugs & Dollars: A Global Challenge." *Freedom Review* 27, no. 4 (July/August 1996): 9–104.

Shannon, Elaine. *Desperadoes: Latin Drug Lords, U.S. Lawmen, and the War America Can't Win.* New York: Viking, 1988.

U.S. Department of State. Bureau for International Narcotics and Law Enforcement Affairs. *International Narcotics Control Strategy Report:* March 1996. Washington, D.C.: Government Printing Office, 1996.

Chapter 4: The Decriminalization of Drugs

Inciardi, James A., and Christine A. Saum. "Legalization Madness." *Public Interest*, no. 123 (Spring 1996): 72–82.

"The War on Drugs Is Lost." *National Review* 48, no. 2 (February 12, 1996): 34–48. (Articles by William F. Buckley, Jr., Ethan A. Nadelmann, Kurt Schmoke, Joseph D. McNamara, Robert W. Sweet, Thomas Szasz, and Steven R. Duke.) See also "400 Readers Give Their Views." *National Review* 48, no. 12 (July 1, 1996): 32–37.

Wilson, James Q. "Against the Legalization of Drugs." *Commentary* 89, no. 2 (February 1990): 21–28. See also "Letters from Readers," *Commentary* 89, no. 5 (May 1990): 4–7, 10–12; and "Letters from Readers," *Commentary* 89, no. 6 (June 1990): 8–11.

Chapter 5: Drug Laws and Civil Liberties

Bovard, James. *Lost Rights: The Destruction of American Liberty*. New York: St. Martin's Press, 1994.

Farley, Terrence P. "Asset Forfeiture Reform: A Law Enforcement Response." *New York Law School Law Review* 39, nos. 1–2 (1994): 149–161.

Hyde, Henry. *Forfeiting Our Property Rights: Is Your Property Safe from Seizure?* Washington, D.C.: Cato Institute, 1995.

Chapter 6: Drugs and Racial Minorities

Kennedy, Randall. "Is Everything Race?" *New Republic* 214, no. 1 (January 1, 1996): 18, 20–21.

Lusane, Clarence. *Pipe Dream Blues: Racism & the War on Drugs*. Boston, MA: South End Press, 1990.

Suro, Roberto, and Walter Pincus. "The CIA and Crack: Evidence Is Lacking of Alleged Plot." *Washington Post*, October 4, 1996, pp. A1, A19.

Wilbanks, William. *The Myth of a Racist Criminal Justice System*. Monterey, CA: Brooks/Cole, 1987.

Chapter 7: Drug Testing

Ligocki, Kenneth B. *Drug Testing: What We All Need to Know*. Bellingham, WA: Scarborough Pub., 1996.

Lipman, Ira A. "Drug Testing Is Vital in the Workplace." *USA Today Magazine* 123, no. 2596 (January 1995): 81–82.

Potter, Beverly A., and J. Sebastian Orfali. *Drug Testing at Work: A Guide for Employers and Employees*. Berkeley, CA: Ronin Publishing, 1990.

Smith, Leef. "If You Want a Job, Better 'Just Say No.'" *Washington Post*, September 18, 1996, pp. A1, A14, A16.

FURTHER READING

Adint, Victor. *Drugs and Crime.* Baltimore, MD: Rosen, 1994

Berger, Gilda. *Crack: The New Drug Epidemic.* Danbury, CT: Watts, 1994

Bernardo, Neal, ed. *The War on Drugs: Opposing Viewpoints.* San Diego, CA: Greenhaven, 1990

Carroll, Marilyn. *Cocaine and Crack.* Springfield, NJ: Enslow, 1994

Clayton, Lawrence. *Drugs and Drug Testing in School.* Baltimore, MD: Rosen, 1996

Draimin, Barbara H. *Drugs and AIDS.* Baltimore, MD: Rosen, 1994

Hawley, Richard. *Drugs and Society.* New York: Walker, 1993

Miller, Maryann. *Drugs and Date Rape.* Baltimore, MD: Rosen, 1995

Oliver, Marilyn T. *Drugs: Should They Be Legalized?* Springfield, NJ: Enslow, 1996

Pascoe, Elaine. *Mexico and the United States: Cooperation and Conflict.* New York: Twenty-First Century, 1996

Rosen, Ruth, ed. *Drugs and Birth Defects.* Baltimore, MD: Rosen, 1995

Schleichert, Elizabeth. *Marijuana.* Springfield, NJ: Enslow, 1996

Swisher, Karin L., and Katie DeKoster, ed. *Drug Abuse: Opposing Viewpoints.* San Diego, CA: Greenhaven, 1994

Washburne, Carolyn K. *Drug Abuse.* San Diego, CA: Lucent, 1996

APPENDIX 1

WHERE YOU CAN GET MORE INFORMATION

Interested in finding out more? You can get free materials from the following organizations and agencies:

African American Family Services
2616 Nicollet Avenue
South Minneapolis, MN 55408
(612) 871-7878

Al-Anon/Alateen Family Group Headquarters, Inc.
P.O. Box 862
Midtown Station
New York, NY 10018-0862
1-800-356-9996

American Council for Drug Education
164 West 75th Street
New York, NY 10023
(212) 595-5810 x7861

Boys & Girls Clubs of America National Headquarters
1230 West Peachtree Street, N.W.
Atlanta, GA 30309
1-404-815-5766

Center for Substance Abuse Treatment Information & Treatment Referral Hotline
1-800-662-HELP or, 1-800-66-AYUDA
(Spanish-speaking callers)

Cocaine Anonymous (CA)
3740 Overland Avenue, Suite C
Los Angeles, CA 90034
1-800-347-8998

Drug Enforcement Administration
Demand Reduction Section
Washington, D.C. 20537
(202) 307-7936

International Institute for Inhalant Abuse
450 West Jefferson Avenue
Englewood, CO 80110
(303) 788-1951

Narcotics Anonymous (NA)
P.O. Box 9999
Van Nuys, CA 91409
(818) 997-3822

National Clearinghouse for Alcohol and Drug Information (NCADT)
P.O. Box 2345
Rockville, MD 20847-2345
1-800-729-6686

National Council of La Raza
1111 19th Street, N.W., Suite 1000
Washington, D.C. 20036
(202) 785-1670

National Council on Alcoholism and Drug Dependence (NCADD)
12 West 21st Street
New York, NY 10010
1-800-622-2255

National Families in Action
2296 Henderson Mill Road, Suite 300
Atlanta, GA 30345
(770) 934-6364

National Inhalant Prevention Coalition
1201 W. 6th Street, Suite C-200
Austin, TX 78703-5252
1-800-269-4237

National Public Information
(Canada)
1-800-714-7498

Don't forget to call your local police department, health department, and local drug prevention organizations for more information on drugs.

INDEX